ROE v. WADE

ROE v. WADE

UNITED STATES SUPREME COURT

Annotated by Bo Schambelan

RUNNING PRESS
PHILADELPHIA, PENNSYLVANIA

The texts of *Roe v. Wade* and *Doe v. Bolton* are from
the *United States Reports,* published by the U. S.
Government Printing Office.

Canadian representatives: General Publishing Co.,
Ltd., 30 Lesmill Road, Don Mills, Ontario M3B 2T6.

International representatives: Worldwide Media
Services, Inc., 30 Montgomery Street, Jersey City,
New Jersey, 07302.

9 8 7 6 5 4 3 2 1
Digit on the right indicates the number of this
printing.

Library of Congress Cataloging-in-publication
Number 92–050330

ISBN 1–56138–202–7

Cover design by Toby Schmidt
Interior design by Robert Perry

Typography: Adobe Garamond, by
COMMCOR Communications Corporation,
Philadelphia, Pennsylvania
Printed in the United States by the Banta Company

This book may be ordered from the publisher.
Please add $2.50 postage and handling.
But try your bookstore first!

Running Press Book Publishers
125 South Twenty-second Street
Philadelphia, Pennsylvania 19103

CONTENTS

INTRODUCTION

Few court cases are as discussed as *Roe v. Wade. Roe* raises difficult issues, issues with legal, moral, and religious implications.

Does a woman have a legal right to an abortion? Is the termination of a pregnancy a decision to be made by a woman and her doctor, or is the protection of potential human life a legitimate interest of a government? At what point does an unborn person acquire legal rights that are protectable under our laws?

The majority, concurring, and dissenting opinions in *Roe* present legal thinking about these and other questions. But no court case exists in a vacuum, and these controversial issues continue to be reviewed and debated in our legal system. The purpose of this book is to make *Roe v. Wade* available and accessible to the reading public. The annotations are designed with this purpose in mind, as an aid to readers of all opinions.

The written opinion *Roe v. Wade* was released by the United States Supreme Court on January 22, 1973. Of the nine Justices who heard the case, seven voted with the majority. Chief Justice Burger and Associate Justices Douglas and Stewart filed concurring opinions. Two Justices, William Rehnquist and Byron White, dissented. Chief Justice Burger assigned the task of writing the majority decision to Justice Harry Blackmun.

The circumstances that led to *Roe* began in 1970 in the state of Texas. An unmarried pregnant woman wanted to terminate her pregnancy, but the laws of Texas made abortion a crime, except when necessary to save the life of the mother. She decided to challenge the Texas abortion law, and the pseudonym "Jane Roe" was created to protect her privacy. She brought her case against Henry Wade, the District Attorney charged with enforcing Texas law in her county.

Jane Roe filed a class action lawsuit brought on behalf of not only herself, a pregnant woman who wanted access to a safe and legal abortion, but also on behalf of all other women in a similar situation. Roe contended that the Texas law, and other state laws that similarly restricted or prohibited abortion, violated rights that she and other women had under the United States Constitution. Roe argued that the state of Texas did not have the right to invade her privacy, which she asserted included her right to decide whether or not to terminate her pregnancy. She also argued that the Constitution gave her rights as an individual that should be free from state interference of this sort, relying on the concept of personal liberty embodied in the Due Process Clause of the Fourteenth Amendment.

Henry Wade argued that the state had a proper interest in protecting both a pregnant woman's health and human life from the moment of conception. He contended that the Texas legislature expressed in clear language that abortion was a crime, except if necessary to save the life of the mother, and that a majority of the states had similar laws. His position was that the government's interest in protecting the health and welfare of all its people included regulating doctors, medical facilities and procedures, including the abortion procedure, and protecting those who were yet unborn.

Roe v. Wade was first heard in a federal court in Texas, and was then appealed directly to the United States Supreme Court. Roe argued for an unconditional right to terminate her pregnancy. Texas argued for an unconditional right to protect unborn human life.

In its majority decision, the Court established that a woman has a constitutionally protected right to decide whether or not to terminate her pregnancy—but not an absolute right. The Court also established that a state does have a legitimate interest in protecting potential human life—but only after a certain point. Yet once that point is reached, a state's interest becomes so strong that it can prohibit abortions altogether, except those necessary to save the life of a mother.

To settle disputes, a court interprets relevant laws, including the Constitution, and examines established precedent. Judges are charged with applying appropriate legal standards to each issue presented in a case. But even a completely "impartial" judge's writing, at some level, reflects his or her own personal history and perspective. A judge is certainly not a "law maker" in the ordinary sense; the responsibility for making new and different laws is understood to be a function of the elected legislature.

In his *Roe* opinion, Justice Blackmun outlined the extensive history of abortion laws from ancient times until the present, and concluded that current abortion restrictions were not, in fact, rooted in thousands of years of history. Blackmun found that according to English common law, on which American law is based, abortions performed before "quickening" (the first recognizable movement of the fetus in utero) were not indictable offenses.

Blackmun did find restrictions to abortions in relatively recent legislative changes dating from the second half of the nineteenth century. Although early nineteenth-century legislation gave different punishments for abortions before and after "quickening," the distinction later disappeared and penalties increased. Some states had less stringent abortion laws at the time of *Roe,* but the majority still had laws like the Texas statute. Blackmun thus concluded that at the time of the drafting of the Constitution and throughout most of the nineteenth century, a woman had a substantially broader right to terminate her pregnancy than she did in most states in 1973.

Blackmun also examined changes in medical procedures. Abortions in the past had been very dangerous. The state had an interest in protecting a woman from such hazardous procedures, which often had high mortality rates. But due to advances in medical technology, modern abortions performed in the earlier stages of pregnancy have become statistically safer than carrying a pregnancy to term and giving birth. Thus, the state no longer had the protection of maternal health as a valid reason to prevent early abortions.

Finally, Blackmun considered the concept of "viability," the ability of a fetus to survive outside of a woman's body. The majority held that a fetus was not an independent, legal person within the meaning of the Fourteenth Amendment. They also held that once the fetus can sustain an independent status—the ability to survive separately—the state then has a greater interest in protecting it. But even this stage of potential life could not be balanced against the actual life or health of the woman. If an abortion were necessary to save her life, it could still be allowed, even after viability.

After examining these issues, the Court provided its opinions. The majority decision granted abortion rights, but not absolute ones. The decision stressed that a state has an important interest in safeguarding health, maintaining medical standards and procedures, and in protecting potential life. A pregnant woman's privacy cannot be isolated, the Court said, and state interest in the maternal health and potentiality of human life becomes significantly involved at certain compelling points.

The majority opinion presented a trimester framework. According to *Roe*, at the beginning of the pregnancy and up to the end of the first trimester, a woman has the right to make private medical decisions with her doctor without interference from the state. During the second trimester, the state's interest in protecting the health of a woman reaches a compelling point, and the state may choose to regulate abortion procedures in ways that are reasonably related to maternal health. For the third trimester—after viability, when a fetus could survive outside of the woman's body—the state's interest in protecting potential life becomes so strong it can ban abortions outright, except those necessary to save the life or health of the mother.

Along with *Roe*, the Court simultaneously decided a companion case from Georgia called *Doe v. Bolton*. The Court made clear that the cases were to be read together. *Doe* struck down portions of Georgia's abortion laws that called for administrative procedures that made abortions more difficult to obtain. The Court reaffirmed in both *Roe* and *Doe* that state laws must be narrowly drawn to reflect legitimate state interests that do not abridge an individual's constitutionally protected rights.

In his concurring opinion to *Doe*, Chief Justice Burger stated: "plainly, the Court today rejects any claim that the Constitution requires abortion on demand." Justice Stewart wrote that the concept of "liberty" guaranteed by the Fourteenth Amendment, as it effects freedom of personal choice in matters of marriage and family life, clearly embraced the right asserted by Jane Roe. Justice Douglas echoed the "right of privacy" of the majority opinion, and further explored the "blessings of liberty" and the impact of these words of the Constitution's Preamble on a woman's decision whether to bear a child.

In their dissenting opinions to *Roe* and *Doe*, Justices White and

Rehnquist strongly disagreed with the majority's decision. In his dissent in *Roe,* Justice Rehnquist questioned the appropriateness of Jane Roe as a plaintiff. He wrote that "liberty is not guaranteed absolutely against deprivation, only against deprivation without due process of law." He did not see a proper application of a "right of privacy." Justice Rehnquist stated his opinion that the Texas abortion statute had a rational relation to a valid state objective. This relation, he wrote, was the traditional test of constitutionality. He also found fault with the majority's application of precedent. Justice Rehnquist, citing the many state statutes which were analogous to the Texas statute, and citing judicial precedent, concluded that the asserted right to abortion was not so rooted in the traditions and conscience of the American people as to be ranked as fundamental.

In a separate dissent, Justice White, joined by Justice Rehnquist, found nothing in the language or history of the Constitution to support the Court's judgment: "The court simply fashions a new constitutional right" as an "exercise of raw judicial power." The issue of whether human life is to be protected or exterminated should, he wrote, be left with the people and to the political and legislative processes the people have designed to govern their aVairs.

The differing views on this controversial topic may never be reconciled, not by philosophers, theologians, or legal or medical thinkers. *Roe v. Wade* provides ways in which to consider complex issues as they continue to be debated, litigated, and reviewed.

—N.A.A.

NOTES ON THE TEXT

This book contains the complete texts of *Roe v. Wade* and *Doe v. Bolton*. Supreme Court opinions provide citations—sometimes lengthy —to laws and legal authorities, including decisions of state and federal courts. An understanding of all of this material is not required to follow the main arguments of the Justices. In the interest of making the opinions more readable, sections of such material have been moved to the Appendix (page 85), where interested readers may refer to it. In the decisions, the removal of text has been noted with brackets and ellipses: [. . . .]. All footnotes are those of the Court.

Some sections of the decisions contain legal language not accessible to the lay reader. Again, such material has been moved to the Appendix, and the removal noted with brackets and ellipses. In the brackets, an effort has been made to summarize accurately the removed material in more accessible language.

A note on citations: All Supreme Court decisions are published in official form in the *United States Reports,* which is available in any law school or bar association library. The Supreme Court uses a uniform method of citation to refer to its previous decisions. For example:

Lochner v. New York, 198 U. S. 45, 76 (1905)

refers to a case decided in the year 1905; it is found in volume 198 of the *United States Reports.* The case begins on page 45, and page 76 contains the material of interest. The citations for the decisions in this book are: *Roe v. Wade,* 410 U. S. 113 (1973), and *Doe v. Bolton,* 410 U. S. 179 (1973).

As an aid to the reader, a Glossary has been included in this book. It contains the legal terms used in the decisions.

ROE ET AL. *v.* WADE, DISTRICT ATTORNEY OF DALLAS COUNTY

Appeal from the United States District Court for the northern district of Texas

No. 70-18. Argued December 13, 1971—Reargued October 11, 1972—Decided January 22, 1973

[. . . . Justice Blackmun delivered the opinion of the Court, in which Chief Justice Burger and Justices Douglas, Brennan, Stewart, Marshall, and Powell joined.

Justice Stewart filed a concurring opinion. Justice Rehnquist filed a dissenting opinion, in which Justice White joined.

The concurring opinions of Chief Justice Burger and Justice Douglas in *Doe v. Bolton* (see page 67) and the dissenting opinion of Justice White, in which Justice Rehnquist joined (see p. 76), also apply to this case.]

MR. JUSTICE BLACKMUN delivered the opinion of the Court.

This Texas federal appeal and its Georgia companion, *Doe v. Bolton, post,* p.[51], present constitutional challenges to state criminal abortion legislation. The Texas statutes under attack here are typical of those that have been in effect in many States for approximately a century. The Georgia statutes, in contrast, have a modern cast and are a legislative product that, to an extent at least, obviously reflects the influences of recent attitudinal change, of advancing medical knowledge and techniques, and of new thinking about an old issue.

We forthwith acknowledge our awareness of the sensitive and emotional nature of the abortion controversy, of the vigorous opposing views, even among physicians, and of the deep and seemingly absolute convictions that the subject inspires. One's philosophy, one's experiences, one's exposure to the raw edges of human existence, one's religious training, one's attitudes toward life and family and their values, and the moral standards one establishes and seeks to observe, are all likely to influence and to color one's thinking and conclusions about abortion.

In addition, population growth, pollution, poverty, and racial overtones tend to complicate and not to simplify the problem.

Our task, of course, is to resolve the issue by constitutional measurement, free of emotion and of predilection. We seek earnestly to do this, and, because we do, we have inquired into, and in this opinion place some emphasis upon, medical and medical-legal history and what that history reveals about man's attitudes toward the abortion procedure over the centuries. We bear in mind, too, Mr. Justice Holmes' admonition in his now-vindicated dissent in *Lochner v. New York,* 198 U. S. 45, 76 (1905):

> "[The Constitution] is made for people of fundamentally differing views, and the accident of our finding certain opinions natural and familiar or novel and even shocking ought not to conclude our judgment upon the question whether statutes embodying them conflict with the Constitution of the United States."

I

The Texas statutes that concern us here are Arts. 1191-1194 and 1196 of the State's Penal Code.[1] These make it a crime to "procure an

---

[1] "Article 191. Abortion

"If any person shall designedly administer to a pregnant woman or knowingly procure to be administered with her consent any drug or medicine, or shall use towards her any violence or means whatever externally or internally applied, and thereby procure an abortion, he shall be confined in the penitentiary not less than two nor more than five years; if it be done without her consent, the punishment shall be doubled. By 'abortion' is meant that the life of the fetus or embryo shall be destroyed in the woman's womb or that a premature birth thereof be caused.

"Art. 1192. Furnishing the means

"Whoever furnishes the means for procuring an abortion knowing the purpose intended is guilty as an accomplice.

"Art. 1193. Attempt at abortion

"If the means used shall fail to produce an abortion, the offender is nevertheless guilty of an attempt abortion," as therein defined, or to attempt one, except with respect to "an abortion procured or attempted by medical advice for the purpose of saving the life of the mother." Similar statutes are in existence in a majority of the States.[2]

Texas first enacted a criminal abortion statute in 1854. [....] This was soon modified into language that has remained substantially unchanged to the present time.

[....All of these statutes] provided the same exception, as does the present Article 1196, for an abortion by "medical advice for the purpose of saving the life of the mother."[3]

II

Jane Roe,[4] a single woman who was residing in Dallas County, Texas, instituted this federal action in March 1970 against the District Attorney of the county. She sought a declaratory judgment that the Texas criminal abortion statutes were unconstitutional on their face, and an injunction restraining the defendant from enforcing the statutes.

Roe alleged that she was unmarried and pregnant; that she wished to terminate her pregnancy by an abortion "performed by a competent, licensed physician, under safe, clinical conditions"; that she was unable to get a "legal" abortion in Texas because her life did not appear to be threatened by the continuation of her pregnancy; and that she

---

to produce abortion, provided it be shown that such means were calculated to produce that result, and shall be fined not less than one hundred nor more than one thousand dollars.

"Art. 1194. Murder in producing abortion

"If the death of the mother is occasioned by an abortion so produced or by an attempt to effect the same it is murder."

"Art. 1196. By medical advice

"Nothing in this chapter applies to an abortion procured or attempted by medical advice for the purpose of saving the life of the mother."

The foregoing Articles, together with Art. 1195, compose Chapter 9 of Title 15 of the Penal Code. Article 1195, not attacked here, reads:

"Art. 1195. Destroying unborn child

"Whoever shall during parturition of the mother destroy the vitality or life in a child in a state of being born and before actual birth, which child would otherwise have been born alive, shall be confined in the penitentiary for life or for not less than five years."

[2][....]

[3][....]

[4] The name is a pseudonym.

could not afford to travel to another jurisdiction in order to secure a legal abortion under safe conditions. She claimed that the Texas statutes were unconstitutionally vague and that they abridged her right of personal privacy, protected by the First, Fourth, Fifth, Ninth, and Fourteenth Amendments. By an amendment to her complaint Roe purported to sue "on behalf of herself and all other women" similarly situated.

James Hubert Hallford, a licensed physician, sought and was granted leave to intervene in Roe's action. In his complaint he alleged that he had been arrested previously for violations of the Texas abortion statutes and that two such prosecutions were pending against him. He described conditions of patients who came to him seeking abortions, and he claimed that for many cases he, as a physician, was unable to determine whether they fell within or outside the exception recognized by Article 1196. He alleged that, as a consequence, the statutes were vague and uncertain, in violation of the Fourteenth Amendment, and that they violated his own and his patients' rights to privacy in the doctor-patient relationship and his own right to practice medicine, rights he claimed were guaranteed by the First, Fourth, Fifth, Ninth, and Fourteenth Amendments.

John and Mary Doe,[5] a married couple, filed a companion complaint to that of Roe. They also named the District Attorney as defendant, claimed like [similar] constitutional deprivations, and sought declaratory and injunctive relief. The Does alleged that they were a childless couple; that Mrs. Doe was suffering from a "neural-chemical" disorder; that her physician had "advised her to avoid pregnancy until such time as her condition has materially improved" (although a pregnancy at the present time would not present "a serious risk" to her life); that, pursuant to medical advice, she had discontinued use of birth control pills; and that if she should become pregnant, she would want to terminate the pregnancy by an abortion performed by a competent, licensed physician under safe, clinical conditions. By an amendment to their complaint, the Does purported to sue "on behalf of themselves and all couples similarly situated."

The two actions were consolidated and heard together by a duly

---

[5] These names are pseudonyms.

convened three-judge district court. The suits thus presented the situations of the pregnant single woman, the childless couple, with the wife not pregnant, and the licensed practicing physician, all joining in the attack on the Texas criminal abortion statutes. [. . . . The District Court held that Dr. Hallford, Roe, and women in her situation had standing to sue, but that the Does did not have standing.] On the merits, the District Court held that the "fundamental right of single women and married persons to choose whether to have children is protected by the Ninth Amendment, through the Fourteenth Amendment," and that the Texas criminal abortion statutes were void on their face because they were both unconstitutionally vague and constituted an overbroad infringement of the plaintiffs' Ninth Amendment rights.

[. . . .The District Court declared the abortion statute void. The District Court applied the doctrine of abstention with respect to the request for injunctive relief. (314f supp. 1217, 1225 n.d. Tex 1970.)

The Does have appealed the dismissal of their complaint. Roe and Dr. Hallford have appealed the District Court's decision not to grant the injunction. The District Attorney filed his own appeal, contending that the statute was Constitutional.]

III

[. . . .]

IV

We are next confronted with issues of justiciability, standing, and abstention [. . . .]

A. *Jane Roe.* Despite the use of the pseudonym, no suggestion is made that Roe is a fictitious person. For purposes of her case, we accept as true, and as established, her existence; her pregnant state, as of the inception of her suit in March 1970 and as late as May 21 of that year when she filed an alias affidavit with the District Court; and her inability to obtain a legal abortion in Texas.

Viewing Roe's case as of the time of its filing and thereafter until as late as May, there can be little dispute that it then presented a case or controversy and that, wholly apart from the class [class-action lawsuit] aspects, she, as a pregnant single woman thwarted by the Texas criminal abortion laws, had standing to challenge those statutes. [. . .]

The appellee [the District Attorney] notes, however, that the record does not disclose that Roe was pregnant at the time of the District Court hearing on May 22, 1970,[6] or on the following June 17 when the court's opinion and judgment were filed. And he suggests that Roe's case must now be moot because she and all other members of her class are no longer subject to any 1970 pregnancy.

[. . . .]

But when, as here, pregnancy is a significant fact in the litigation, the normal 266-day human gestation period is so short that the pregnancy will come to term before the usual appellate process is complete. If that termination makes a case moot, pregnancy litigation seldom will survive much beyond the trial stage, and appellate review will be effectively denied. Our law should not be that rigid. Pregnancy often comes more than once to the same woman, and in the general population, if man is to survive, it will always be with us. [. . . .The usual rule is that an appeal cannot continue if the controversy no longer exists. But exceptions are made for controversies which are repetitious and yet would always evade appellate review. Pregnancy is a classic example of such a controversy.]

We, therefore, agree with the District Court that Jane Roe had standing to undertake this litigation, that she presented a justiciable controversy, and that the termination of her 1970 pregnancy has not rendered her case moot.

B. *Dr. Hallford.* The doctor's position is different. He entered Roe's litigation as a plaintiff-intervenor, alleging in his complaint that he:

"[I]n the past has been [twice] arrested for violating the Texas Abortion Laws and at the present time stands charged by indictment with violating said laws in the Criminal District Court of Dallas County, Texas. In both cases the defendant is charged with abortion [. . . .]

Although he stated that he has been arrested in the past for violating the State's abortion laws, he makes no allegation of any substantial and immediate threat to any federally protected right that cannot be asserted in his defense against the state prosecutions.

---

[6] [. . . .]

Neither is there any allegation of harassment or bad-faith prosecution. [. . . . The rule is that federal courts will not interfere with a criminal prosecution in a state court unless there is a claim of harassment or bad faith prosecution. Dr. Hallford may raise his defenses, based on the Constitution, in the criminal case in Texas.][7]

C. *The Does.* [. . . .] Their pleadings present them as a childless married couple, the woman not being pregnant, who have no desire to have children at this time because of their having received medical advice that Mrs. Doe should avoid pregnancy, and for "other highly personal reasons." But they "fear . . . they may face the prospect of becoming parents." And if pregnancy ensues, they "would want to terminate" it by an abortion. They assert an inability to obtain an abortion legally in Texas and, consequently, the prospect of obtaining an illegal abortion there or of going outside Texas to some place where the procedure could be obtained legally and competently.

We thus have as plaintiffs a married couple who have, as their asserted immediate and present injury, only an alleged "detrimental effect upon [their] marital happiness" because they are forced to "the choice of refraining from normal sexual relations or of endangering Mary Doe's health through a possible pregnancy." Their claim is that sometime in the future Mrs. Doe might become pregnant because of possible failure of contraceptive measures, and at that time in the future she might want an abortion that might then be illegal under the Texas statutes.

This very phrasing of the Does' position reveals its speculative character. Their alleged injury rests on possible future contraceptive failure, possible future pregnancy, possible future unpreparedness for parenthood, and possible future impairment of health. Any one or more of these several possibilities may not take place and all may not combine. In the Does' estimation, these possibilities might have some real or imagined impact upon their marital happiness. But we are not prepared to say that the bare allegation of so indirect an injury is sufficient to present an actual case or controversy. [. . . .]

The Does therefore are not appropriate plaintiffs in this litigation. Their complaint was properly dismissed by the District Court, and we

---

[7][. . . .]

affirm that dismissal. [The dismissal of their complaint has little significance, since Roe has standing and has attacked the same statutes with essentially the same claims.]

V

The principal thrust of appellant's attack on the Texas statutes is that they improperly invade a right, said to be possessed by the pregnant woman, to choose to terminate her pregnancy. Appellant would discover this right in the concept of personal "liberty" embodied in the Fourteenth Amendment's Due Process Clause; or in personal, marital, familial, and sexual privacy said to be protected by the Bill of Rights or its penumbras, see *Griswold v. Connecticut*, 381 U. S. 479 (1965); *Eisenstadt v. Baird*, 405 U. S. 438 (1972); *id.*, at 460 (WHITE, J., concurring in result); or among those rights reserved to the people by the Ninth Amendment, *Griswold v. Connecticut*, 381 U. S. at 486 (Goldberg, J., concurring). Before addressing this claim, we feel it desirable briefly to survey, in several aspects, the history of abortion, for such insight as that history may afford us, and then to examine the state purposes and interests behind the criminal abortion laws.

VI

It perhaps is not generally appreciated that the restrictive criminal abortion laws in effect in a majority of States today are of relatively recent vintage. Those laws, generally proscribing abortion or its attempt at any time during pregnancy except when necessary to preserve the pregnant woman's life, are not of ancient or even of common-law origin. Instead, they derive from statutory changes effected, for the most part, in the latter half of the 19th century.

1. *Ancient attitudes.* These are not capable of precise determination. We are told that at the time of the Persian Empire abortifacients were known and that criminal abortions were severely punished.[8] We are also told, however, that abortion was practiced in Greek times as well as in the Roman Era,[9] and that "it was resorted to without scruple."[10] The Ephesian, Soranos, often described as the greatest of the ancient gynecologists, appears to have been generally opposed to

---

8, 9, 10 [. . . .]

Rome's prevailing free-abortion practices. He found it necessary to think first of the life of the mother, and he resorted to abortion when, upon this standard, he felt the procedure advisable.[11] Greek and Roman law afforded little protection to the unborn. If abortion was prosecuted in some places, it seems to have been based on a concept of a violation of the father's right to his offspring. Ancient religion did not bar abortion.[12]

2. The Hippocratic Oath. What then of the famous Oath that has stood so long as the ethical guide of the medical profession and that bears the name of the great Greek (460(?)-377(?) B. C.), who has been described as the Father of Medicine, the "wisest and the greatest practitioner of his art," and the "most important and most complete medical personality of antiquity," who dominated the medical schools of his time, and who typified the sum of the medical knowledge of the past?[13] The Oath varies somewhat according to the particular transla-tion, but in any translation the content is clear: "I will give no deadly medicine to anyone if asked, nor suggest any such counsel; and in like manner I will not give to a woman a pessary to produce abortion,"[14] or "I will neither give a deadly drug to anybody if asked for it, nor will I make a suggestion to this effect. Similarly, I will not give to a woman an abortive remedy."[15]

Although the Oath is not mentioned in any of the principal briefs in this case or in *Doe v. Bolton*, [p. 51], it represents the apex of the development of strict ethical concepts in medicine, and its influence endures to this day. Why did not the authority of Hippocrates dissuade abortion practice in his time and that of Rome? The late Dr. Edelstein provides us with a theory:[16] The Oath was not uncontested even in Hippocrates' day; only the Pythagorean school of philosophers frowned upon the related act of suicide. Most Greek thinkers, on the other hand, commended abortion, at least prior to viability. See Plato, Republic, V, 461; Aristotle, Politics, VII, 1335b 25. For the Pythagoreans, however, it was a matter of dogma. For them the embryo was animate from the moment of conception, and abortion meant destruction of a living being. The abortion clause of the Oath, therefore, "echoes Pythagorean doctrines," and "[i]n no other stratum

11, 12, 13, 14, 15, 16 [. . .]

of Greek opinion were such views held or proposed in the same spirit of uncompromising austerity."[17]

Dr. Edelstein then concludes that the Oath originated in a group representing only a small segment of Greek opinion and that it certainly was not accepted by all ancient physicians. He points out that medical writings down to Galen (A. D. 130-200) "give evidence of the violation of almost every one of its injunctions."[18] But with the end of antiquity a decided change took place. Resistance against suicide and against abortion became common. The Oath came to be popular. The emerging teachings of Christianity were in agreement with the Pythagorean ethic. The Oath "became the nucleus of all medical ethics" and "was applauded as the embodiment of truth." Thus, suggests Dr. Edelstein, it is "a Pythagorean manifesto and not the expression of an absolute standard of medical conduct."[19]

This, it seems to us, is a satisfactory and acceptable explanation of the Hippocratic Oath's apparent rigidity. It enables us to understand, in historical context, a long-accepted and revered statement of medical ethics.

3. *The common law.* It is undisputed that at common law, abortion performed before "quickening"—the first recognizable movement of the fetus *in utero,* appearing usually from the 16th to the 18th week of pregnancy[20]—was not an indictable offense.[21] The absence of a common-law crime for pre-quickening abortion appears to have developed from a confluence of earlier philosophical, theological, and civil and canon law concepts of when life begins. These disciplines variously approached the question in terms of the point at which the embryo or fetus became "formed" or recognizably human, or in terms of when a "person" came into being, that is, infused with a "soul" or "animated." A loose consensus evolved in early English law that these events occurred at some point between conception and live birth.[22] This was "mediate animation." Although Christian theology and the canon law came to fix the point of animation at 40 days for a male and 80 days for a female, a view that persisted until the 19th century, there was otherwise little agreement about the precise time of formation or animation. There was agreement, however, that prior to this point the

---

17, 18, 19, 20, 21, 22 [. . . .]

fetus was to be regarded as part of the mother, and its destruction, therefore, was not homicide. Due to continued uncertainty about the precise time when animation occurred, to the lack of any empirical basis for the 40-80-day view, and perhaps to Aquinas' definition of movement as one of the two first principles of life, Bracton focused upon quickening as the critical point. The significance of quickening was echoed by later common-law scholars and found its way into the received common law in this country.

Whether abortion of a *quick* fetus was a felony at common law, or even a lesser crime, is still disputed. Bracton, writing early in the 13th century, thought it homicide.[23] But the later and predominant view, following the great common-law scholars, has been that it was, at most, a lesser offense. In a frequently cited passage, Coke took the position that abortion of a woman "quick with childe" is "a great misprision, and no murder."[24] Blackstone followed, saying that while abortion after quickening had once been considered manslaughter (though not murder), "modern law" took a less severe view.[25] A recent review of the common-law precedents argues, however, that those precedents contradict Coke and that even post-quickening abortion was never established as a common-law crime.[26] This is of some importance because while most American courts ruled, in holding or dictum, that abortion of an unquickened fetus was not criminal under their received common law,[27] others followed Coke in stating that abortion of a quick fetus was a "misprision," a term they translated to mean "misdemeanor."[28] That their reliance on Coke on this aspect of

---

23, 24, 25 [. . . .]

26Means, The Phoenix of Abortional Freedom: Is a Penumbral or Ninth-Amendment Right About to Arise from the Nineteenth-Century Legislative Ashes of a Fourteenth-Century Common-Law Liberty?, 17 N. Y. L. F. 335 (1971) (hereinafter Means II). The author examines the two principal precedents cited marginally by Coke, both contrary to his dictum, and traces the treatment of these and other cases by earlier commentators. He concludes that Coke, who himself participated as an advocate in an abortion case in 1601, may have intentionally misstated the law. The author even suggests a reason: Coke's strong feelings against abortion, coupled with his determination to assert common-law (secular) jurisdiction to assess penalties for an offense that traditionally had been an exclusively ecclesiastical or canon-law crime. See also Lader 78-79, who notes that some scholars doubt that the common law ever was applied to abortion: that the English ecclesiastical courts seem to have lost interest in the problem after 1527: and that the preamble to the English legislation of 1803, 43 Geo. 3, c. 58, § 1. referred to in the text, *infra*, at 136, states that "no adequate means have been hitherto provided for the prevention and punishment of such offenses."

27, 28 [. . . .]

the law was uncritical and, apparently in all the reported cases, dictum (due probably to the paucity of common-law prosecutions for post-quickening abortion), makes it now appear doubtful that abortion was ever firmly established as a common-law crime even with respect to the destruction of a quick fetus.

4. *The English statutory law.* England's first criminal abortion statute, Lord Ellenborough's Act, [. . .] came in 1803. It made abortion of a quick fetus, § 1, a capital crime, but in § 2 it provided lesser penalties for the felony of abortion before quickening, and thus preserved the "quickening" distinction. This contrast was continued in the general revision of 1828, [. . . .] It disappeared, however, together with the death penalty, in 1837, 7 Will. 4 & 1 Vict., c. 85, § 6, and did not reappear in the Offenses Against the Person Act of 1861, [. . .], that formed the core of English anti-abortion law until the liberalizing reforms of 1967. In 1929, the Infant Life (Preservation) Act, [. . .] came into being. Its emphasis was upon the destruction of "the life of a child capable of being born alive." It made a willful act performed with the necessary intent a felony. It contained a proviso that one was not to be found guilty of the offense "unless it is proved that the act which caused the death of the child was not done in good faith for the purpose only of preserving the life of the mother."

A seemingly notable development in the English law was the case of *Rex v. Bourne,* [1939] [. . . .] This case apparently answered in the affirmative the question whether an abortion necessary to preserve the life of the pregnant woman was excepted from the criminal penalties of the 1861 Act. In his instructions to the jury, Judge Macnaghten referred to the 1929 Act, and observed that that Act related to "the case where a child is killed by a wilful act at the time when it is being delivered in the ordinary course of nature." *Id.,* at 691. He concluded that the 1861 Act's use of the word "unlawfully," imported the same meaning expressed by the specific proviso in the 1929 Act, even though there was no mention of preserving the mother's life in the 1861 Act. He then construed the phrase "preserving the life of the mother" broadly, that is, "in a reasonable sense," to include a serious and permanent threat to the mother's *health,* and instructed the jury to acquit Dr. Bourne if it found he had acted in a good-faith belief that the abortion was necessary for this purpose. *Id.,* at 693-694. The jury did acquit.

Recently, Parliament enacted a new abortion law. This is the Abortion Act of 1967, [. . . .] The Act permits a licensed physician to perform an abortion where two other licensed physicians agree (a) "that the continuance of the pregnancy would involve risk to the life of the pregnant woman, or of injury to the physical or mental health of the pregnant woman or any existing children of her family, greater than if the pregnancy were terminated," or (b) "that there is a substantial risk that if the child were born it would suffer from such physical or mental abnormalities as to be seriously handicapped." The Act also provides that, in making this determination, "account may be taken of the pregnant woman's actual or reasonably foreseeable environment." It also permits a physician, without the concurrence of others, to terminate a pregnancy where he is of the good-faith opinion that the abortion "is immediately necessary to save the life or to prevent grave permanent injury to the physical or mental health of the pregnant woman."

5. *The American law.* In this country, the law in effect in all but a few States until mid-19th century was the pre-existing English common law. Connecticut, the first State to enact abortion legislation, adopted in 1821 that part of Lord Ellenborough's Act that related to a woman "quick with child."[29] The death penalty was not imposed. Abortion before quickening was made a crime in that State only in 1860.[30] In 1828, New York enacted legislation[31] that, in two respects, was to serve as a model for early anti-abortion statutes. First, while barring destruction of an unquickened fetus as well as a quick fetus, it made the former only a misdemeanor, but the latter second-degree manslaughter. Second, it incorporated a concept of therapeutic abortion by providing that an abortion was excused if it "shall have been necessary to preserve the life of such mother, or shall have been advised by two physicians to be necessary for such purpose." By 1840, when Texas had received the common law,[32] only eight American States had statutes dealing with abortion.[33] It was not until after the War Between the States that legislation began generally to replace the common law. Most of these initial statutes dealt severely with abortion after quickening but were lenient with it before quickening. Most punished attempts equally with completed abortions. While many

29, 30, 31, 32, 33 [. . .]

25

statutes included the exception for an abortion thought by one or more physicians to be necessary to save the mother's life, that provision soon disappeared and the typical law required that the procedure actually be necessary for that purpose.

Gradually, in the middle and late 19th century the quickening distinction disappeared from the statutory law of most States and the degree of the offense and the penalties were increased. By the end of the 1950's, a large majority of the jurisdictions banned abortion, however and whenever performed, unless done to save or preserve the life of the mother.[34] The exceptions, Alabama and the District of Columbia, permitted abortion to preserve the mother's health.[35] Three States permitted abortions that were not "unlawfully" performed or that were not "without lawful justification," leaving interpretation of those standards to the courts.[36] In the past several years, however, a trend toward liberalization of abortion statutes has resulted in adoption, by about one-third of the States, of less stringent laws, most of them patterned after the ALI Model Penal Code, § 230.3,[37] set forth as Appendix B to the opinion in *Doe v. Bolton,* [p. 51].

It is thus apparent that at common law, at the time of the adoption of our Constitution, and throughout the major portion of the 19th century, abortion was viewed with less disfavor than under most American statutes currently in effect. Phrasing it another way, a woman enjoyed a substantially broader right to terminate a pregnancy than she does in most States today. At least with respect to the early stage of pregnancy, and very possibly without such a limitation, the opportunity to make this choice was present in this country well into

---

[34] Criminal abortion statutes in effect in the States as of 1961, together with historical statutory development and important judicial interpretations of the state statutes, are cited and quoted in Quay 447-520. See Comment, A Survey of the Present Statutory and Case Law on Abortion: The Contradictions and the Problems, 1972 U. Ill. L. F. 177, 179, classifying the abortion statutes and listing 25 States as permitting abortion only if necessary to save or preserve the mother's life.

[35,36] [. . . .]

[37] Fourteen States have adopted some form of the ALI statute [. . . .] Mr. Justice Clark described some of these States as having "led the way." Religion, Morality, and Abortion: A Constitutional Appraisal, 2 Loyola U. (L.A.) L. Rev. 1, 11 (1969).

By the end of 1970, four other States had repealed criminal penalties for abortions performed in early pregnancy by a licensed physician, subject to stated procedural and health requirements [. . . .] The precise status of criminal abortion laws in some States is made unclear by recent decisions in state and federal courts striking down existing state laws, in whole or in part.

the 19th century. Even later, the law continued for some time to treat less punitively an abortion procured in early pregnancy.

6. *The position of the American Medical Association.* The anti-abortion mood prevalent in this country in the late 19th century was shared by the medical profession. Indeed, the attitude of the profession may have played a significant role in the enactment of stringent criminal abortion legislation during that period.

An AMA Committee on Criminal Abortion was appointed in May 1857. It presented its report, 12 Trans. of the Am. Med. Assn. 73–78 (1859), to the Twelfth Annual Meeting. That report observed that the Committee had been appointed to investigate criminal abortion "with a view to its general suppression." It deplored abortion and its frequency and it listed three causes of "this general demoralization":

"The first of these causes is a wide-spread popular ignorance of the true character of the crime—a belief, even among mothers themselves, that the foetus is not alive till after the period of quickening.

"The second of the agents alluded to is the fact that the profession themselves are frequently supposed careless of foetal life . . . .

"The third reason of the frightful extent of this crime is found in the grave defects of our laws, both common and statute, as regards the independent and actual existence of the child before birth, as a living being. These errors, which are sufficient in most instances to prevent conviction, are based, and only based, upon mistaken and exploded medical dogmas. With strange inconsistency, the law fully acknowledges the foetus in utero and its inherent rights, for civil purposes; while personally and as criminally affected, it fails to recognize it, and to its life as yet denies all protection." *Id.,* at 75–76.

The Committee then offered, and the Association adopted, resolutions protesting "against such unwarrantable destruction of human life," calling upon state legislatures to revise their abortion laws, and requesting the cooperation of state medical societies "in pressing the subject." *Id.,* at 28, 78.

In 1871 a long and vivid report was submitted by the Committee on Criminal Abortion. It ended with the observation, "We had to deal with human life. In a matter of less importance we could entertain no compromise. An honest judge on the bench would call things by their proper names. We could do no less." 22 Trans. of the Am. Med. Assn. 258 (1871). It proffered resolutions, adopted by the Association, *id.,* at 38–39, recommending, among other things, that it "be unlawful and unprofessional for any physician to induce abortion or premature labor, without the concurrent opinion of at least one respectable consulting physician, and then always with a view to the safety of the child—if that be possible," and calling "the attention of the clergy of all denominations to the perverted views of morality entertained by a large class of females—aye, and men also, on this important question."

Except for periodic condemnation of the criminal abortionist, no further formal AMA action took place until 1967. In that year, the Committee on Human Reproduction urged the adoption of a stated policy of opposition to induced abortion, except when there is "documented medical evidence" of a threat to the health or life of the mother, or that the child "may be born with incapacitating physical deformity or mental deficiency," or that a pregnancy "resulting from legally established statutory or forcible rape or incest may constitute a threat to the mental or physical health of the patient," two other physicians "chosen because of their recognized professional competence have examined the patient and have concurred in writing," and the procedure "is performed in a hospital accredited by the Joint Commission of Accreditation of Hospitals." The providing of medical information by physicians to state legislatures in their consideration of legislation regarding therapeutic abortion was "to be considered consistent with the principles of ethics of the American Medical Association." This recommendation was adopted by the House of Delegates. Proceedings of the AMA House of Delegates 40-51 (June 1967).

In 1970, after the introduction of a variety of proposed resolutions, and of a report from its Board of Trustees, a reference committee noted "polarization of the medical profession on this controversial issue"; division among those who had testified; a difference of opinion among AMA councils and committees; "the remarkable shift in testimony" in six months, felt to be influenced "by the rapid changes in state laws and by the judicial decisions which tend to make abortion more freely available;"

and a feeling "that this trend will continue." On June 25, 1970, the House of Delegates adopted preambles and most of the resolutions proposed by the reference committee. The preambles emphasized "the best interests of the patient," "sound clinical judgment," and "informed patient consent," in contrast to "mere acquiescence to the patient's demand." The resolutions asserted that abortion is a medical procedure that should be performed by a licensed physician in an accredited hospital only after consultation with two other physicians and in conformity with state law, and that no party to the procedure should be required to violate personally held moral principles.[38] Proceedings of the AMA House of Delegates 220 (June 1970). The AMA Judicial Council rendered a complementary opinion.[39]

7. *The position of the American Public Health Association.* In October 1970, the Executive Board of the APHA adopted Standards for Abortion Services. These were five in number:

"a. Rapid and simple abortion referral must be readily available through state and local public health departments, medical societies, or other non-profit organizations.

"b. An important function of counseling should be to simplify and expedite the provision of abortion services; it should not delay the obtaining of these services.

"c. Psychiatric consultation should not be mandatory. As in the case of other specialized medical services, psychiatric consultation should be sought for definite indications and not on a routine basis.

"d. A wide range of individuals from appropriately trained, sympathetic volunteers to highly skilled physicians may qualify as abortion counselors.

"e. Contraception and/or sterilization should be discussed with each abortion patient." Recommended Standards for Abortion Services, 61 Am. J. Pub. Health 396 (1971).

---

[38] [. . . .]

[39] "The Principles of Medical Ethics of the AMA do not prohibit a physician from performing an abortion that is performed in accordance with good medical practice and under circumstances that do not violate the laws of the community in which he practices.

"In the matter of abortions, as of any other medical procedure, the Judicial Council becomes involved whenever there is alleged violation of the Principles of Medical Ethics as established by the House of Delegates."

Among factors pertinent to life and health risks associated with abortion were three that "are recognized as important":

"a. the skill of the physician,

"b. the environment in which the abortion is performed, and above all

"c. the duration of pregnancy, as determined by uterine size and confirmed by menstrual history." *Id.,* at 397.

It was said that "a well-equipped hospital" offers more protection "to cope with unforeseen difficulties than an office or clinic without such resources. . . . The factor of gestational age is of overriding importance." Thus, it was recommended that abortions in the second trimester and early abortions in the presence of existing medical complications be performed in hospitals as inpatient procedures. For pregnancies in the first trimester, abortion in the hospital with or without overnight stay "is probably the safest practice." An abortion in an extramural facility, however, is an acceptable alternative "provided arrangements exist in advance to admit patients promptly if unforeseen complications develop." Standards for an abortion facility were listed. It was said that at present abortions should be performed by physicians or osteopaths who are licensed to practice and who have "adequate training." *Id.,* at 398.

8. *The position of the American Bar Association.* At its meeting in February 1972 the ABA House of Delegates approved, with 17 opposing votes, the Uniform Abortion Act that had been drafted and approved the preceding August by the Conference of Commissioners on Uniform State Laws. 58 A. B. A. J. 380 (1972). We set forth the Act in full in the margin.[40] The Conference has appended an enlightening Prefatory Note.[41]

[40] [. . . .]

[41] "This Act is based largely upon the New York abortion act following a review of the more recent laws on abortion in several states and upon recognition of a more liberal trend in laws on this subject. Recognition was given also to the several decisions in state and federal courts which show a further trend toward liberalization of abortion laws, especially during the first trimester of pregnancy.

"Recognizing that a number of problems appeared in New York, a shorter time period for 'unlimited' abortions was advisable. The time period was bracketed to permit the various states to insert a figure more in keeping with the different conditions that might exist among the states. Likewise, the language limiting the place or places in which abortions may be performed was also bracketed to account for different conditions among the states. In addition, limitations on abortions after the initial 'unlimited' period were placed in brackets so that individual states may adopt all or any of these reasons, or place further restrictions upon abortions after the initial period.

VII

Three reasons have been advanced to explain historically the enactment of criminal abortion laws in the 19th century and to justify their continued existence.

It has been argued occasionally that these laws were the product of a Victorian social concern to discourage illicit sexual conduct. Texas, however, does not advance this justification in the present case, and it appears that no court or commentator has taken the argument seriously.[42] The appellants and *amici* contend, moreover, that this is not a proper state purpose at all and suggest that, if it were, the Texas statutes are overbroad in protecting it since the law fails to distinguish between married and unwed mothers.

A second reason is concerned with abortion as a medical procedure. When most criminal abortion laws were first enacted, the procedure was a hazardous one for the woman.[43] This was particularly true prior to the development of antisepsis. Antiseptic techniques, of course, were based on discoveries by Lister, Pasteur, and others first announced in 1867, but were not generally accepted and employed until about the turn of the century. Abortion mortality was high. Even after 1900, and perhaps until as late as the development of antibiotics in the 1940's, standard modern techniques such as dilation and curettage were not nearly so safe as they are today. Thus, it has been argued that a State's real concern in enacting a criminal abortion law was to protect the pregnant woman, that is, to restrain her from submitting to a procedure that placed her life in serious jeopardy.

Modern medical techniques have altered this situation. Appellants and various *amici* refer to medical data indicating that abortion in early pregnancy, that is, prior to the end of the first trimester, although not without its risk, is now relatively safe. Mortality rates for women undergoing early abortions, where the procedure is legal,

"This Act does not contain any provision relating to medical review committees or prohibitions against sanctions imposed upon medical personnel refusing to participate in abortions because of religious or other similar reasons, or the like. Such provisions, while related, do not directly pertain to when, where, or by whom abortions may be performed; however, the Act is not drafted to exclude such a provision by a state wishing to enact the same."

42,43,44 [....]

appear to be as low as or lower than the rates for normal childbirth.[44] Consequently, any interest of the State in protecting the woman from an inherently hazardous procedure, except when it would be equally dangerous for her to forgo it, has largely disappeared. Of course, important state interests in the areas of health and medical standards do remain. The State has a legitimate interest in seeing to it that abortion, like any other medical procedure, is performed under circumstances that insure maximum safety for the patient. This interest obviously extends at least to the performing physician and his staff, to the facilities involved, to the availability of after-care, and to adequate provision for any complication or emergency that might arise. The prevalence of high mortality rates at illegal "abortion mills" strengthens, rather than weakens, the State's interest in regulating the conditions under which abortions are performed. Moreover, the risk to the woman increases as her pregnancy continues. Thus, the State retains a definite interest in protecting the woman's own health and safety when an abortion is proposed at a late stage of pregnancy.

The third reason is the State's interest—some phrase it in terms of duty—in protecting prenatal life. Some of the argument for this justification rests on the theory that a new human life is present from the moment of conception.[45] The State's interest and general obligation to protect life then extends, it is argued, to prenatal life. Only when the life of the pregnant mother herself is at stake, balanced against the life she carries within her, should the interest of the embryo or fetus not prevail. Logically, of course, a legitimate state interest in this area need not stand or fall on acceptance of the belief that life begins at conception or at some other point prior to live birth. In assessing the State's interest, recognition may be given to the less rigid claim that as long as at least *potential* life is involved, the State may assert interests beyond the protection of the pregnant woman alone.

Parties challenging state abortion laws have sharply disputed in some courts the contention that a purpose of these laws, when enacted, was to protect prenatal life.[46] Pointing to the absence of legislative history to support the contention, they claim that most state laws were designed solely to protect the woman. Because medical advances have

45,46 [....]

lessened this concern, at least with respect to abortion in early pregnancy, they argue that with respect to such abortions the laws can no longer be justified by any state interest. There is some scholarly support for this view of original purpose.[47] The few state courts called upon to interpret their laws in the late 19th and early 20th centuries did focus on the State's interest in protecting the woman's health rather than in preserving the embryo and fetus.[48] Proponents of this view point out that in many States, including Texas,[49] by statute or judicial interpretation, the pregnant woman herself could not be prosecuted for self-abortion or for cooperating in an abortion performed upon her by another.[50] They claim that adoption of the "quickening" distinction through received common law and state statutes tacitly recognizes the greater health hazards inherent in late abortion and impliedly repudiates the theory that life begins at conception.

It is with these interests, and the weight to be attached to them, that this case is concerned.

VIII

The Constitution does not explicitly mention any right of privacy. In a line of decisions, however, going back perhaps as far as *Union Pacific R. Co. v. Botsford,* 141 U. S. 250, 251 (1891), the Court has recognized that a right of personal privacy, or a guarantee of certain areas or zones of privacy, does exist under the Constitution. In varying contexts, the Court or individual Justices have, indeed, found at least the roots of that right in the First Amendment, *Stanley v. Georgia,* 394 U. S. 557, 564 (1969); in the Fourth and Fifth Amendments, *Terry v. Ohio,* 392 U. S. 1, 8–9 (1968), *Katz v. United States,* 389 U. S. 347, 350 (1967), *Boyd v. United States,* 116 U. S. 616 (1886), see *Olmstead v. United States,* 277 U. S. 438, 478 (1928) (Brandeis, J., dissenting); in the penumbras of the Bill of Rights, *Griswold v. Connecticut,* 381 U. S., at 484–485; in the Ninth Amendment, *id.,* at 486 (Goldberg, J., concurring); or in the concept of liberty guaranteed by the first section of the Fourteenth Amendment, see *Meyer v. Nebraska,* 262 U. S. 390,

---

[47,48] [. . . .]

[49] [. . . .] There is no immunity in Texas for the father who is not married to the mother. [. . . .]

[50] [. . . .]

399 (1923). These decisions make it clear that only personal rights that can be deemed "fundamental" or "implicit in the concept of ordered liberty," *Palko v. Connecticut,* 302 U. S. 319, 325 (1937), are included in this guarantee of personal privacy. They also make it clear that the right has some extension to activities relating to marriage, *Loving v. Virginia,* 388 U. S. 1, 12 (1967); procreation, *Skinner v. Oklahoma,* 316 U. S. 535, 541–542 (1942); contraception, *Eisenstadt v. Baird,* 405 U. S., at 453–454; *id.,* at 460, 463–465 (WHITE, J., concurring in result); family relationships, *Prince v. Massachusetts,* 321 U. S. 158, 166 (1944); and child rearing and education, *Pierce v. Society of Sisters,* 268 U. S. 510, 535 (1925), *Meyer v. Nebraska, supra.*

This right of privacy, whether it be founded in the Fourteenth Amendment's concept of personal liberty and restrictions upon state action, as we feel it is, or, as the District Court determined, in the Ninth Amendment's reservation of rights to the people, is broad enough to encompass a woman's decision whether or not to terminate her pregnancy. The detriment that the State would impose upon the pregnant woman by denying this choice altogether is apparent. Specific and direct harm medically diagnosable even in early pregnancy may be involved. Maternity, or additional offspring, may force upon the woman a distressful life and future. Psychological harm may be imminent. Mental and physical health may be taxed by child care. There is also the distress, for all concerned, associated with the unwanted child, and there is the problem of bringing a child into a family already unable, psychologically and otherwise, to care for it. In other cases, as in this one, the additional difficulties and continuing stigma of unwed motherhood may be involved. All these are factors the woman and her responsible physician necessarily will consider in consultation.

On the basis of elements such as these, appellant and some *amici* argue that the woman's right is absolute and that she is entitled to terminate her pregnancy at whatever time, in whatever way, and for whatever reason she alone chooses. With this we do not agree. Appellant's arguments that Texas either has no valid interest at all in regulating the abortion decision, or no interest strong enough to support any limitation upon the woman's sole determination, are unpersuasive. The Court's decisions recognizing a right of privacy also acknowledge that some state regulation in areas protected by that right is appropriate. As noted above, a State may properly assert important interests in safeguarding health, in maintaining medical standards, and in protecting potential life. At some point in pregnancy, these respective interests become sufficiently compelling to sustain regulation of the factors that govern the abortion decision. The privacy right involved, therefore, cannot be said to be absolute. In fact, it is not clear to us that the claim asserted by some *amici* that one has an unlimited right to do with one's body as one pleases bears a close relationship to the right of privacy previously articulated in the Court's decisions. The Court has refused to recognize an unlimited right of this kind in the past. *Jacobson v. Massachusetts,* 197 U. S. 11 (1905) (vaccination); *Buck v. Bell,* 274 U. S. 200 (1927) (sterilization).

We, therefore, conclude that the right of personal privacy includes the abortion decision, but that this right is not unqualified and must be considered against important state interests in regulation.

We note that those federal and state courts that have recently considered abortion law challenges have reached the same conclusion. A majority, in addition to the District Court in the present case, have held state laws unconstitutional, at least in part, because of vagueness or because of overbreadth and abridgment of rights. [. . . . The states were Connecticut, Georgia, Illinois, Kansas, New Jersey, Wisconsin, California, Florida.]

Others have sustained state statutes. [. . . . Kentucky, Louisiana, North Carolina, Ohio, Utah, Indiana, Mississippi, South Dakota.]

Although the results are divided, most of these courts have agreed that the right of privacy, however based, is broad enough to cover the abortion decision; that the right, nonetheless, is not absolute and is subject to some limitations; and that at some point the state interests as to protection of health, medical standards, and prenatal life, become dominant. We agree with this approach.

Where certain "fundamental rights" are involved, the Court has held that regulation limiting these rights may be justified only by a "compelling state interest." *Kramer v. Union Free School District,* 395 U. S. 621, 627 (1969; *Shapiro v. Thompson,* 394 U. S. 618, 634 (1969), *Sherbert v. Verner,* 374 U. S. 398, 406 (1963), and that legislative enactments must be narrowly drawn to express only the legitimate state interests at stake. *Griswold v. Connecticut,* 381 U. S., at 485; *Aptheker v. Secretary of State,* 378 U. S. 500, 508 (1964); *Cantwell v. Connecticut,* 310 U. S. 296, 307-308 (1940); see *Eisenstadt v. Baird,* 405 U. S., at 460, 463–464 (WHITE, J., concurring in result).

In recent abortion cases, cited above, courts have recognized these principles. Those striking down state laws have generally scrutinized the State's interests in protecting health and potential life, and have concluded that neither interest justified broad limitations on the reasons for which a physician and his pregnant patient might decide that she should have an abortion in the early stages of pregnancy. Courts sustaining state laws have held that the State's determinations to protect health or prenatal life are dominant and constitutionally justifiable.

IX

The District Court held that the appellee [the District Attorney] failed to meet his burden of demonstrating that the Texas statute's infringement upon Roe's rights was necessary to support a compelling state interest, and that, although the appellee presented "several compelling justifications for state presence in the area of abortions," the statutes outstripped these justifications and swept "far beyond any areas of compelling state interest." 314 F. Supp., at 1222–1223. Appellant [Roe] and appellee [the District Attorney] both contest that holding. Appellant, as has been indicated, claims an absolute right that bars any state imposition of criminal penalties in the area. Appellee argues that the State's determination to recognize and protect prenatal life from and after conception constitutes a compelling state interest. As noted above , we do not agree fully with either formulation.

A. The appellee [the District Attorney] and certain *amici* argue that the fetus is a "person" within the language and meaning of the Fourteenth Amendment. In support of this, they outline at length and in detail the well-known facts of fetal development. If this suggestion of personhood is established, the appellant's [Roe's] case, of course, collapses, for the fetus' right to life would then be guaranteed specifically by the Amendment. The appellant [Roe] conceded as

[51] [. . . .]

much on reargument.[51] On the other hand, the appellee [the District Attorney] conceded on reargument[52] that no case could be cited that holds that a fetus is a person within the meaning of the Fourteenth Amendment.

The Constitution does not define "person" in so many words. Section 1 of the Fourteenth Amendment contains three references to "person." The first, in defining "citizens," speaks of "persons born or naturalized in the United States." The word also appears both in the Due Process Clause and in the Equal Protection Clause. "Person" is used in other places in the Constitution: in the listing of qualifications for Representatives and Senators, Art. I, § 2 cl. 2, and § 3, cl. 3; in the Apportionment Clause, Art. I, § 2, cl. 3;[53] in the Migration and Importation provision. Art. I, § 9, cl. 1; in the Emolument Clause, Art. I, § 9, cl. 8; in the Electors provisions. Art. II. § 1, cl. 2, and the superseded cl. 3; in the provision outlining qualifications for the office of President, Art. II, § 1, cl. 5; in the Extradition provisions, Art. IV, § 2, cl. 2, and the superseded Fugitive Slave Clause 3; and in the Fifth, Twelfth, and Twenty-second Amendments, as well as in §§ 2 and 3 of the Fourteenth Amendment. But in nearly all these instances, the use of the word is such that it has application only postnatally. None indicates, with any assurance, that it has any possible pre-natal application.[54]

All this, together with our observation, *supra,* that throughout the major portion of the 19th century prevailing legal abortion practices

---

[52] [. . . .]

[53] We are not aware that in the taking of any census under this clause, a fetus has ever been counted.

[54] When Texas urges that a fetus is entitled to Fourteenth Amendment protection as a person, it faces a dilemma. Neither in Texas nor in any other State are all abortions prohibited. Despite broad proscription, an exception always exists. The exception contained in Art. 1196, for an abortion procured or attempted by medical advice for the purpose of saving the life of the mother, is typical. But if the fetus is a person who is not to be deprived of life without due process of law, and if the mother's condition is the sole determinant, does not the Texas exception appear to be out of line with the Amendment's command?

There are other inconsistencies between Fourteenth Amendment status and the typical abortion statute. It has already been pointed out, n. 49, *supra,* that in Texas the woman is not a principal or an accomplice with respect to an abortion upon her. If the fetus is a person, why is the woman not a principal or an accomplice? Further, the penalty for criminal abortion specified by Art. 1195 is significantly less than the maximum penalty for murder prescribed by Art. 1257 of the Texas Penal Code. If the fetus is a person, may the penalties be different?

were far freer than they are today, persuades us that the word "person," as used in the Fourteenth Amendment, does not include the unborn.[55] This is in accord with the results reached in those few cases where the issue has been squarely presented. [. . . .] Indeed, our decision in *United States v. Vuitch*, 402 U. S. 62 (1971), inferentially is to the same effect, for we there would not have indulged in statutory interpretation favorable to abortion in specified circumstances if the necessary consequence was the termination of life entitled to Fourteenth Amendment protection.

This conclusion, however, does not of itself fully answer the contentions raised by Texas, and we pass on to other considerations.

B. The pregnant woman cannot be isolated in her privacy. She carries an embryo and, later, a fetus, if one accepts the medical definitions of the developing young in the human uterus. See Dorland's Illustrated Medical Dictionary 478–479, 547 (24th ed. 1965). The situation therefore is inherently different from marital intimacy, or bedroom possession of obscene material, or marriage, or procreation, or education, with which *Eisenstadt* and *Griswold, Stanley, Loving, Skinner,* and *Pierce* and *Meyer* were respectively concerned. As we have intimated above, it is reasonable and appropriate for a State to decide that at some point in time another interest, that of health of the mother or that of potential human life, becomes significantly involved. The woman's privacy is no longer sole and any right of privacy she possesses must be measured accordingly.

Texas urges that, apart from the Fourteenth Amendment, life begins at conception and is present throughout pregnancy, and that, therefore, the State has a compelling interest in protecting that life from and after conception. We need not resolve the difficult question of when life begins. When those trained in the respective disciplines of medicine, philosophy, and theology are unable to arrive at any consensus, the judiciary, at this point in the development of man's knowledge, is not in a position to speculate as to the answer.

It should be sufficient to note briefly the wide divergence of

---

[55] Cf. the Wisconsin abortion statute, defining "unborn child" to mean "a human being from the time of conception until it is born alive," Wis. Stat. § 940.04 (6) (1969), and the new Connecticut statute, Pub. Act No. 1 (May 1972 special session), declaring it to be the public policy of the State and the legislative intent "to protect and preserve human life from the moment of conception."

thinking on this most sensitive and difficult question. There has always been strong support for the view that life does not begin until live birth. This was the belief of the Stoics.[56] It appears to be the predominant, though not the unanimous, attitude of the Jewish faith.[57] It may be taken to represent also the position of a large segment of the Protestant community, insofar as that can be ascertained; organized groups that have taken a formal position on the abortion issue have generally regarded abortion as a matter for the conscience of the individual and her family.[58] As we have noted, the common law found greater significance in quickening. Physicians and their scientific colleagues have regarded that event with less interest and have tended to focus either upon conception, upon live birth, or upon the interim point at which the fetus becomes "viable," that is, potentially able to live outside the mother's womb, albeit with artificial aid.[59] Viability is usually placed at about seven months (28 weeks) but may occur earlier, even at 24 weeks.[60] The Aristotelian theory of "mediate animation," that held sway throughout the Middle Ages and the Renaissance in Europe, continued to be official Roman Catholic dogma until the 19th century, despite opposition to this "ensoulment" theory from those in the Church who would recognize the existence of life from the moment of conception.[61] The latter is now, of course, the official belief of the Catholic Church. As one brief *amicus* discloses, this is a view strongly held by many non-Catholics as well, and by many physicians. Substantial problems for precise definition of this view are posed, however, by new embryological data that purport to indicate that conception is a "process" over time, rather than an event, and by new medical techniques such as menstrual extraction, the "morning-after" pill, implantation of embryos, artificial insemination, and even artificial wombs.[62]

In areas other than criminal abortion, the law has been reluctant to endorse any theory that life, as we recognize it, begins before live birth or to accord legal rights to the unborn except in narrowly defined situations and except when the rights are contingent upon live birth. For example, the traditional rule of tort law denied recovery for prenatal injuries even though the child was born alive.[63] That rule has

---

56, 57, 58, 59, 60, 61, 62, 63 [. . . .]

been changed in almost every jurisdiction. In most States, recovery is said to be permitted only if the fetus was viable, or at least quick, when the injuries were sustained, though few courts have squarely so held.[64] In a recent development, generally opposed by the commentators, some States permit the parents of a stillborn child to maintain an action for wrongful death because of prenatal injuries.[65] Such an action, however, would appear to be one to vindicate the parents' interest and is thus consistent with the view that the fetus, at most, represents only the potentiality of life. Similarly, unborn children have been recognized as acquiring rights or interests by way of inheritance or other devolution of property, and have been represented by guardians *ad litem.*[66] Perfection of the interests involved, again, has generally been contingent upon live birth. In short, the unborn have never been recognized in the law as persons in the whole sense.

X

In view of all this, we do not agree that, by adopting one theory of life, Texas may override the rights of the pregnant woman that are at stake. We repeat, however, that the State does have an important and legitimate interest in preserving and protecting the health of the pregnant woman, whether she be a resident of the State or a nonresident who seeks medical consultation and treatment there, and that it has still *another* important and legitimate interest in protecting the potentiality of human life. These interests are separate and distinct. Each grows in substantiality as the woman approaches term and, at a point during pregnancy, each becomes "compelling."

With respect to the State's important and legitimate interest in the health of the mother, the "compelling" point, in the light of present medical knowledge, is at approximately the end of the first trimester. This is so because of the now-established medical fact, referred to above at [page 31], that until the end of the first trimester mortality in abortion may be less than mortality in normal childbirth. It follows that, from and after this point, a State may regulate the abortion procedure to the extent that the regulation reasonably relates to the preservation and protection of maternal health. Examples of permis-

---

64, 65, 66 [. . . .]

sible state regulation in this area are requirements as to the qualifications of the person who is to perform the abortion; as to the licensure of that person; as to the facility in which the procedure is to be performed, that is, whether it must be a hospital or may be a clinic or some other place of less-than-hospital status; as to the licensing of the facility; and the like.

This means, on the other hand, that, for the period of pregnancy prior to this "compelling" point, the attending physician, in consultation with his patient, is free to determine, without regulation by the State, that, in his medical judgment, the patient's pregnancy should be terminated. If that decision is reached, the judgment may be effectuated by an abortion free of interference by the State.

With respect to the State's important and legitimate interest in potential life, the "compelling" point is at viability. This is so because the fetus then presumably has the capability of meaningful life outside the mother's womb. State regulation protective of fetal life after viability thus has both logical and biological justifications. If the State is interested in protecting fetal life after viability, it may go so far as to proscribe abortion during that period, except when it is necessary to preserve the life or health of the mother.

Measured against these standards, Art. 1196 of the Texas Penal Code, in restricting legal abortions to those "procured or attempted by medical advice for the purpose of saving the life of the mother," sweeps too broadly. The statute makes no distinction between abortions performed early in pregnancy and those performed later, and it limits to a single reason, "saving" the mother's life, the legal justification for the procedure. The statute, therefore, cannot survive the constitutional attack made upon it here.

This conclusion makes it unnecessary for us to consider the additional challenge to the Texas statute asserted on grounds of vagueness. See *United States v. Vuitch,* 402 U. S., at 67-72.

XI

To summarize and to repeat:

1. A state criminal abortion statute of the current Texas type, that excepts from criminality only a life-saving procedure on behalf of the mother, without regard to pregnancy stage and without recognition of

the other interests involved, is violative of the Due Process Clause of the Fourteenth Amendment.

(a) For the stage prior to approximately the end of the first trimester, the abortion decision and its effectuation must be left to the medical judgment of the pregnant woman's attending physician.

(b) For the stage subsequent to approximately the end of the first trimester, the State, in promoting its interest in the health of the mother, may, if it chooses, regulate the abortion procedure in ways that are reasonably related to maternal health.

(c) For the stage subsequent to viability, the State in promoting its interest in the potentiality of human life may, if it chooses, regulate, and even proscribe, abortion except where it is necessary, in appropriate medical judgment, for the preservation of the life or health of the mother.

2. The State may define the term "physician," as it has been employed in the preceding paragraphs of this Part XI of this opinion, to mean only a physician currently licensed by the State, and may proscribe any abortion by a person who is not a physician as so defined.

In *Doe v. Bolton,* [page 51] procedural requirements contained in one of the modern abortion statutes are considered. That opinion and this one, of course, are to be read together.[67]

This holding, we feel, is consistent with the relative weights of the respective interests involved, with the lessons and examples of medical and legal history, with the lenity of the common law, and with the demands of the profound problems of the present day. The decision leaves the State free to place increasing restrictions on abortion as the period of pregnancy lengthens, so long as those restrictions are tailored to the recognized state interests. The decision vindicates the right of the physician to administer medical treatment according to his professional judgment up to the points where important state interests provide compelling justifications for intervention. Up to those points,

---

[67] Neither in this opinion nor in *Doe v. Bolton, post.* p. 51, do we discuss the father's rights, if any exist in the constitutional context, in the abortion decision. No paternal right has been asserted in either of the cases, and the Texas and the Georgia statutes on their face take no cognizance of the father. We are aware that some statutes recognize the father under certain circumstances. North Carolina, for example, N. C. Gen. Stat. § 14-45.1 (Supp. 1971), requires written permission for the abortion from the husband when the woman is a married minor, that is, when she is less than 18 years of age, 41 N. C. A. G. 489 (1971); if the woman is an unmarried minor, written permission from the parents is required. We need not now decide whether provisions of this kind are constitutional.

the abortion decision in all its aspects is inherently, and primarily, a medical decision, and basic responsibility for it must rest with the physician. If an individual practitioner abuses the privilege of exercising proper medical judgment, the usual remedies, judicial and intra-professional, are available.

XII

Our conclusion that Art. 1196 is unconstitutional means, of course, that the Texas abortion statutes, as a unit, must fall. The exception of Art. 1196 [the exception which permits an abortion to save the life of the mother] cannot be struck down separately, for then the State would be left with a statute proscribing all abortion procedures no matter how medically urgent the case.

Although the District Court granted appellant Roe declaratory relief, it stopped short of issuing an injunction against enforcement of the Texas statutes. [. . . .]

We find it unnecessary to decide whether the District Court erred in withholding injunctive relief, for we assume the Texas prosecutorial authorities will give full credence to this decision that the present criminal abortion statutes of that State are unconstitutional.

The judgment of the District Court as to intervenor Hallford is reversed, and Dr. Hallford's complaint in intervention is dismissed. In all other respects, the judgment of the District Court is affirmed. Costs are allowed to the appellee.

It is so ordered.

Mr. Justice Stewart, concurring.

In 1963, this Court, in *Ferguson v. Skrupa,* 372 U. S. 726, purported to sound the death knell for the doctrine of substantive due process, a doctrine under which many state laws had in the past been held to violate the Fourteenth Amendment. As Mr. Justice Black's opinion for the Court in *Skrupa* put it: "We have returned to the original constitutional proposition that courts do not substitute their social and economic beliefs for the judgment of legislative bodies, who are elected to pass laws." *Id.,* at 730.[1]

---

[1] Only Mr. Justice Harlan failed to join the Court's opinion, 372 U. S., at 733.

Barely two years later, in *Griswold v. Connecticut,* 381 U. S. 479, the Court held a Connecticut birth control law unconstitutional. In view of what had been so recently said in *Skrupa,* the Court's opinion in *Griswold* understandably did its best to avoid reliance on the Due Process Clause of the Fourteenth Amendment as the ground for decision. Yet, the Connecticut law did not violate any provision of the Bill of Rights, nor any other specific provision of the Constitution.[2] So it was clear to me then, and it is equally clear to me now, that the *Griswold* decision can be rationally understood only as a holding that the Connecticut statute substantively invaded the "liberty" that is protected by the Due Process Clause of the Fourteenth Amendment.[3] As so understood, *Griswold* stands as one in a long line of pre-*Skrupa* cases decided under the doctrine of substantive due process, and I now accept it as such.

"In a Constitution for a free people, there can be no doubt that the meaning of 'liberty' must be broad indeed." *Board of Regents v. Roth,* 408 U. S. 564, 572. The Constitution nowhere mentions a specific right of personal choice in matters of marriage and family life, but the "liberty" protected by the Due Process Clause of the Fourteenth Amendment covers more than those freedoms explicitly named in the Bill of Rights. See *Schware v. Board of Bar Examiners,* 353 U. S. 232, 238-239; *Pierce v. Society of Sisters,* 268 U. S. 510, 534-535; *Meyer v. Nebraska,* 262 U. S. 390, 399-400. Cf. *Shapiro v. Thompson,* 394 U. S. 618, 629-630; *United States v. Guest,* 383 U. S. 745, 757-758; *Carrington v. Rash,* 380 U. S. 89, 96; *Aptheker v. Secretary of State,* 378 U. S. 500, 505; *Kent v. Dulles,* 357 U. S. 116, 127; *Bolling v. Sharpe,* 347 U. S. 497, 499-500; *Truax v. Raich,* 239 U. S. 33, 41.

As Mr. Justice Harlan once wrote: "[T]he full scope of the liberty

---

[2] There is no constitutional right of privacy, as such. "[The Fourth] Amendment protects individual privacy against certain kinds of governmental intrusion, but its protections go further, and often have nothing to do with privacy at all. Other provisions of the Constitution protect personal privacy from other forms of governmental invasion. But the protection of a person's *general* right to privacy—his right to be let alone by other people—is, like the protection of his property and of his very life, left largely to the law of the individual States." *Katz v. United States,* 389 U. S. 347, 350-351 (footnotes omitted).

[3] This was also clear to Mr. Justice Black, 381 U. S., at 507 (dissenting opinion); to Mr. Justice Harlan, 381 U. S., at 499 (opinion concurring in the judgment); and to MR. JUSTICE WHITE, 381 U. S., at 502 (opinion concurring in the judgment). See also Mr. Justice Harlan's thorough and thoughtful opinion dissenting from dismissal of the appeal in *Poe v. Ullman,* 367 U. S. 497, 522.

guaranteed by the Due Process Clause cannot be found in or limited by the precise terms of the specific guarantees elsewhere provided in the Constitution. This 'liberty' is not a series of isolated points pricked out in terms of the taking of property; the freedom of speech, press, and religion; the right to keep and bear arms; the freedom from unreasonable searches and seizures; and so on. It is a rational continuum which, broadly speaking, includes a freedom from all substantial arbitrary impositions and purposeless restraints . . . and which also recognizes, what a reasonable and sensitive judgment must, that certain interests require particularly careful scrutiny of the state needs asserted to justify their abridgment." *Poe v. Ullman,* 367 U. S. 497, 543 (opinion dissenting from dismissal of appeal) (citations omitted). In the words of Mr. Justice Frankfurter, "Great concepts like . . . 'liberty' . . . were purposely left to gather meaning from experience. For they relate to the whole domain of social and economic fact, and the statesmen who founded this Nation knew too well that only a stagnant society remains unchanged." *National Mutual Ins. Co. v. Tidewater Transfer Co.,* 337 U. S. 582, 646 (dissenting opinion).

Several decisions of this Court make clear that freedom of personal choice in matters of marriage and family life is one of the liberties protected by the Due Process Clause of the Fourteenth Amendment. *Loving v. Virginia,* 388 U. S. 1, 12; *Griswold v. Connecticut, supra; Pierce v. Society of Sisters, supra; Meyer v. Nebraska, supra.* See also *Prince v. Massachusetts,* 321 U. S. 158, 166; *Skinner v. Oklahoma,* 316 U. S. 535, 541. As recently as last Term, in *Eisenstadt v. Baird,* 405 U. S. 438, 453, we recognized "the right of the *individual,* married or single, to be free from unwarranted governmental intrusion into matters so fundamentally affecting a person as the decision whether to bear or beget a child." That right necessarily includes the right of a woman to decide whether or not to terminate her pregnancy. "Certainly the interests of a woman in giving of her physical and emotional self during pregnancy and the interests that will be affected throughout her life by the birth and raising of a child are of a far greater degree of significance and personal intimacy than the right to send a child to private school protected in Pierce v. Society of Sisters, 268 U. S. 510 (1925), or the right to teach a foreign language protected in Meyer v. Nebraska, 262 U. S. 390 (1923)." *Abele v. Markle,* 351 F. Supp. 224, 227 (Conn. 1972).

Clearly, therefore, the Court today is correct in holding that the right asserted by Jane Roe is embraced within the personal liberty protected by the Due Process Clause of the Fourteenth Amendment.

It is evident that the Texas abortion statute infringes that right directly. Indeed, it is difficult to imagine a more complete abridgment of a constitutional freedom than that worked by the inflexible criminal statute now in force in Texas. The question then becomes whether the state interests advanced to justify this abridgment can survive the "particularly careful scrutiny" that the Fourteenth Amendment here requires.

The asserted state interests are protection of the health and safety of the pregnant woman, and protection of the potential future human life within her. These are legitimate objectives, amply sufficient to permit a State to regulate abortions as it does other surgical procedures, and perhaps sufficient to permit a State to regulate abortions more stringently or even to prohibit them in the late stages of pregnancy. But such legislation is not before us, and I think the Court today has thoroughly demonstrated that these state interests cannot constitutionally support the broad abridgment of personal liberty worked by the existing Texas law. Accordingly, I join the Court's opinion holding that that law is invalid under the Due Process Clause of the Fourteenth Amendment.

MR. JUSTICE REHNQUIST, dissenting.

The Court's opinion brings to the decision of this troubling question both extensive historical fact and a wealth of legal scholarship. While the opinion thus commands my respect, I find myself nonetheless in fundamental disagreement with those parts of it that invalidate the Texas statute in question, and therefore dissent.

I

The Court's opinion decides that a State may impose virtually no restriction on the performance of abortions during the first trimester of pregnancy. Our previous decisions indicate that a necessary predicate for such an opinion is a plaintiff who was in her first trimester of pregnancy at some time during the pendency of her lawsuit. While a party may vindicate his own constitutional rights, he may not seek vindication for the rights of others. *Moose Lodge v. Irvis,* 407 U. S. 163

(1972); *Sierra Club v. Morton*, 405 U. S. 727 (1972). The Court's statement of facts in this case makes clear, however, that the record in no way indicates the presence of such a plaintiff. We know only that plaintiff Roe at the time of filing her complaint was a pregnant woman; for aught that appears in this record, she may have been in her *last* trimester of pregnancy as of the date the complaint was filed.

Nothing in the Court's opinion indicates that Texas might not constitutionally apply its proscription of abortion as written to a woman in that stage of pregnancy. Nonetheless, the Court uses her complaint against the Texas statute as a fulcrum for deciding that States may impose virtually no restrictions on medical abortions performed during the *first* trimester of pregnancy. In deciding such a hypothetical lawsuit, the Court departs from the longstanding admonition that it should never "formulate a rule of constitutional law broader than is required by the precise facts to which it is to be applied." *Liverpool, New York & Philadelphia S. S. Co. v. Commissioners of Emigration*, 113 U. S. 33, 39 (1885). See also *Ashwander v. TVA*, 297 U. S. 288. 345 (1936) (Brandeis, J., concurring).

II

Even if there were a plaintiff in this case capable of litigating the issue which the Court decides, I would reach a conclusion opposite to that reached by the Court. I have difficulty in concluding, as the Court does, that the right of "privacy" is involved in this case. Texas, by the statute here challenged, bars the performance of a medical abortion by a licensed physician on a plaintiff such as Roe. A transaction resulting in an operation such as this is not "private" in the ordinary usage of that word. Nor is the "privacy" that the Court finds here even a distant relative of the freedom from searches and seizures protected by the Fourth Amendment to the Constitution, which the Court has referred to as embodying a right to privacy. *Katz v. United States*, 389 U. S. 347 (1967).

If the Court means by the term "privacy" no more than that the claim of a person to be free from unwanted state regulation of consensual transactions may be a form of "liberty" protected by the Fourteenth Amendment, there is no doubt that similar claims have been upheld in our earlier decisions on the basis of that liberty. I agree with the statement of MR. JUSTICE STEWART in his concurring opinion that the "liberty," against deprivation of which without due process the Fourteenth Amendment protects, embraces more than the rights found in the Bill of Rights. But that liberty is not guaranteed absolutely against deprivation, only against deprivation without due process of law. The test traditionally applied in the area of social and economic legislation is whether or not a law such as that challenged has a rational relation to a valid state objective. *Williamson v. Lee Optical Co.,* 348 U. S. 483, 491 (1955). The Due Process Clause of the Fourteenth Amendment undoubtedly does place a limit, albeit a broad one, on legislative power to enact laws such as this. If the Texas statute were to prohibit an abortion even where the mother's life is in jeopardy, I have little doubt that such a statute would lack a rational relation to a valid state objective under the test stated in *Williamson, supra.* But the Court's sweeping invalidation of any restrictions on abortion during the first trimester is impossible to justify under that standard, and the conscious weighing of competing factors that the Court's opinion apparently substitutes for the established test is far more appropriate to a legislative judgment than to a judicial one.

The Court eschews the history of the Fourteenth Amendment in its reliance on the "compelling state interest" test. See *Weber v. Aetna Casualty & Surety Co.,* 406 U. S. 164, 179 (1972) (dissenting opinion). But the Court adds a new wrinkle to this test by transposing it from the legal considerations associated with the Equal Protection Clause of the Fourteenth Amendment to this case arising under the Due Process Clause of the Fourteenth Amendment. Unless I misapprehend the consequences of this transplanting of the "compelling state interest test," the Court's opinion will accomplish the seemingly impossible feat of leaving this area of the law more confused than it found it.

While the Court's opinion quotes from the dissent of Mr. Justice Holmes in *Lochner v. New York,* 198 U. S. 45, 74 (1905), the result it reaches is more closely attuned to the majority opinion of Mr. Justice Peckham in that case. As in *Lochner* and similar cases applying substantive due process standards to economic and social welfare legislation, the adoption of the compelling state interest standard will inevitably require this Court to examine the legislative policies and pass on the wisdom of these policies in the very process of deciding whether a particular state interest put forward may or may not be "compelling." The decision here to break pregnancy into three distinct terms and to outline the permissible restrictions the State may impose in each one, for example, partakes more of judicial legislation that it does of a determination of the intent of the drafters of the Fourteenth Amendment.

The fact that a majority of the States reflecting, after all, the majority sentiment in those States, have had restrictions on abortions for at least a century is a strong indication, it seems to me, that the asserted right to an abortion is not "so rooted in the traditions and conscience of our people as to be ranked as fundamental," *Snyder v. Massachusetts,* 291 U. S. 97, 105 (1934). Even today, when society's views on abortion are changing, the very existence of the debate is evidence that the "right" to an abortion is not so universally accepted as the appellant would have us believe.

To reach its result, the Court necessarily has had to find within the scope of the Fourteenth Amendment a right that was apparently completely unknown to the drafters of the Amendment. As early as 1821, the first state law dealing directly with abortion was enacted by the Connecticut Legislature. Conn. Stat., Tit. 22, §§ 14, 16. By the time of the adoption of the Fourteenth Amendment in 1868, there were at least 36 laws enacted by state or territorial legislatures limiting abortion.[1] While many States have amended or updated their laws, 21 of the laws on the books in 1868 remain in effect today.[2] Indeed, the Texas statute struck down today was, as the majority notes, first enacted in 1857 and "has remained substantially unchanged to the present time." *Ante,* at 119.

There apparently was no question concerning the validity of this provision or of any of the other state statutes when the Fourteenth Amendment was adopted. The only conclusion possible from this history is that the drafters did not intend to have the Fourteenth Amendment withdraw from the States the power to legislate with respect to this matter.

[1,2] [. . .]

III

Even if one were to agree that the case that the Court decides were here, and that the enunciation of the substantive constitutional law in the Court's opinion were proper, the actual disposition of the case by the Court is still diYcult to justify. The Texas statute is struck down *in toto,* even though the Court apparently concedes that at later periods of pregnancy Texas might impose these selfsame statutory limitations on abortion. My understanding of past practice is that a statute found to be invalid as applied to a particular plaintiV, but not unconstitutional as a whole, is not simply "struck down" but is, instead, declared unconstitutional as applied to the fact situation before the Court. *Yick Wo v. Hopkins,* 118 U. S. 356 (1886); *Street v. New York,* 394 U. S. 576 (1969).

For all of the foregoing reasons, I respectfully dissent.

DOE ET AL. V. BOLTON, ATTORNEY GENERAL OF GEORGIA, ET AL.

APPEAL FROM THE UNITED STATES DISTRICT COURT FOR THE NORTHERN DISTRICT OF GEORGIA

No.70–40. Argued December 13, 1971—Reargued October 11, 1972
—Decided January 22, 1973

[. . . .]

[. . . . Justice Blackmun delivered the opinion of the Court, in which Chief Justice Burger and Justices Douglas, Brennan, Stewart, Marshall, and Powell joined.

The concurring opinions of Chief Justice Burger and Justice Douglas, and the dissenting opinion of Justice White (in which Justice Rehnquist joined) apply also to *Roe v. Wade.* Justice Rehnquist filed a dissenting opinion.]

MR. JUSTICE BLACKMUN delivered the opinion of the Court.

In this appeal, the criminal abortion statutes recently enacted in Georgia are challenged on constitutional grounds. The statutes are §§ 26–1201 through 26–1203 of the State's Criminal Code, formulated by Georgia Laws, 1968 Session, pp. 1249, 1277–1280. In *Roe v. Wade,* [p. 13], we today have struck down, as constitutionally defective, the Texas criminal abortion statutes that are representative of provisions long in effect in a majority of our States. The Georgia legislation, however, is different and merits separate consideration.

I

The statutes in question are reproduced as Appendix A, [page 79].[1] As the appellants acknowledge,[2] the 1968 statutes are patterned upon the American Law Institute's Model Penal Code, § 230.3 (Proposed Official Draft, 1962), reproduced as Appendix B [page 82]. The ALI proposal has served as the model for recent legislation in approximately one-fourth of our States.[3] The new Georgia provisions replaced statutory law that had been in effect for more than 90 years. Georgia Laws 1876. No 130, § 2, at 113.[4] The predecessor statute paralleled the Texas legislation considered in *Roe v. Wade, supra,* and made all abortions criminal except those necessary "to preserve the life" of the pregnant woman. The new statutes have not been tested on constitutional grounds in the Georgia state courts.

Section 26–1201, with a referenced exception, makes abortion a crime, and § 26–1203 provides that a person convicted of that crime shall be punished by imprisonment for not less than one nor more than 10 years. Section 26–1202 (a) states the exception and removes from § 1201's definition of criminal abortion, and thus makes noncriminal an abortion "performed by a physician duly licensed" in Georgia when, "based upon his best clinical judgment . . . an abortion is necessary because:

"(1) A continuation of the pregnancy would endanger the life of the pregnant woman or would seriously and permanently injure her health; or

"(2) The fetus would very likely be born with a grave, permanent, and irremediable mental or physical defect; or

"(3) The pregnancy resulted from forcible or statutory rape."[5]

Section 26–1202 also requires, by numbered subdivisions of its subsection (b) that, for an abortion to be authorized or performed as a noncriminal procedure, additional conditions must be fulfilled. These are (1) and (2) residence of the woman in Georgia; (3) reduction to writing of the performing physician's medical judgment that an

---

[1,2] [. . . .]

[3,4] [. . . .]

[5] In contrast with the ALI model, the Georgia statute makes no specific reference to pregnancy resulting from incest. We were assured by the State at reargument that this was because the statute's reference to "rape" was intended to include incest. Tr. of Oral Rearg. 32.

abortion is justified for one or more of the reasons specified by § 26–1202 (a), with written concurrence in that judgment by at least two other Georgia-licensed physicians, based upon their separate personal medical examinations of the woman; (4) performance of the abortion in a hospital licensed by the State Board of Health and also accredited by the Joint Commission of Accreditation of Hospitals; (5) advance approval by an abortion committee of not less than three members of the hospital's staff; (6) certifications in a rape situation; and (7), (8), and (9) maintenance and confidentiality of records. There is a provision (subsection (c)) for judicial determination of the legality of a proposed abortion on petition of the judicial circuit law officer or of a close relative, as therein defined, of the unborn child, and for expeditious hearing of that petition. There is also a provision (subsection (e)) giving a hospital the right not to admit an abortion patient and giving any physician and any hospital employee or staff member the right, on moral or religious grounds, not to participate in the procedure.

II

On April 16, 1970, Mary Doe,[6] 23 other individuals (nine described as Georgia-licensed physicians, seven as nurses registered in the State, five as clergymen, and two as social workers), and two nonprofit Georgia corporations that advocate abortion reform instituted this federal action in the Northern District of Georgia against the State's attorney general, the district attorney of Fulton County, and the chief of police of the city of Atlanta. The plaintiffs sought a declaratory judgment that the Georgia abortion statutes were unconstitutional in their entirety. They also sought injunctive relief restraining the defendants and their successors from enforcing the statutes.

Mary Doe alleged:

(1) She was a 22-year-old Georgia citizen, married, and nine weeks pregnant. She had three living children. The two older ones had been placed in a foster home because of Doe's poverty and inability to care for them. The youngest, born July 19, 1969, had been placed for adoption. Her husband had recently abandoned her and she was

---

[6] Appellants by their complaint, App. 7, allege that the name is a pseudonym.

forced to live with her indigent parents and their eight children. She and her husband, however, had become reconciled. He was a construction worker employed only sporadically. She had been a mental patient at the State Hospital. She had been advised that an abortion could be performed on her with less danger to her health than if she gave birth to the child she was carrying. She would be unable to care for or support the new child.

(2) On March 25, 1970, she applied to the Abortion Committee of Grady Memorial Hospital, Atlanta, for a therapeutic abortion under § 26–1202. Her application was denied 16 days later, on April 10, when she was eight weeks pregnant, on the ground that her situation was not one described in § 26–1202 (a).[7]

(3) Because her application was denied, she was forced either to relinquish "her right to decide when and how many children she will bear" or to seek an abortion that was illegal under the Georgia statutes. This invaded her rights of privacy and liberty in matters related to family, marriage, and sex, and deprived her of the right to choose whether to bear children. This was a violation of rights guaranteed her by the First, Fourth, Fifth, Ninth, and Fourteenth Amendments. The statutes also denied her equal protection and procedural due process and, because they were unconstitutionally vague, deterred hospitals and doctors from performing abortions. She sued "on her own behalf and on behalf of all others similarly situated."

The other plaintiffs alleged that the Georgia statutes "chilled and deterred" them from practicing their respective professions and deprived them of rights guaranteed by the First, Fourth, and Fourteenth Amendments. These plaintiffs also purported to sue on their own behalf and on the behalf of others similarly situated.

A three-judge district court was convened. An offer of proof as to Doe's identity was made, but the court deemed it unnecessary to receive proof.

[. . . . The Court held that of the plaintiffs, only Mary Doe was a proper person to seek a judgment. . . .[8]] The court concluded that the

---

[7] In answers to interrogatories, Doe stated that her application for an abortion was approved at Georgia Baptist Hospital on May 5, 1970, but that she was not approved as a charity patient there and had no money to pay for an abortion. App. 64.

[8] [. . . .]

limitation in the Georgia statute of the "number of reasons for which an abortion may be sought," *id.*, at 1056, improperly restricted Doe's rights of privacy articulated in *Griswold v. Connecticut*, 381 U. S. 479 (1965), and of "personal liberty," both of which it thought "broad enough to include the decision to abort a pregnancy," 319 F. Supp., at 1055. As a consequence, the court held invalid those portions of §§ 26–1202 (a)and (b) (3) limiting legal abortions to the three situations specified; § 26–1202 (b) (6) relating to certifications in a rape situation; and § 26–1202 (c) authorizing a court test. Declaratory relief was granted accordingly. The court, however, held that Georgia's interest in protection of health, and the existence of a "*potential* of independent human existence*" (emphasis in original), *id.*, at 1055, justified state regulation of "the manner of performance as well as the quality of the final decision to abort," *id.*, at 1056, and it refused to strike down the other provisions of the statutes. It denied the request for an injunction, *id.*, at 1057.

Claiming that they were entitled to an injunction and to broader relief, the plaintiffs took a direct appeal. [. . . . Defendants, the Attorney General, the District Attorney of Fulton County, and the Chief of Police of the City of Atlanta have taken an appeal which is pending in the Federal Court of Appeals for the Fifth Circuit. What we decide today obviously has implications for the issues raised by defendants in that appeal.]

III

Our decision in *Roe v. Wade, ante,* p. 113, establishes (1) that, despite her pseudonym, we may accept as true, for this case, Mary Doe's existence and her pregnant state on April 16, 1970; (2) that the constitutional issue is substantial; (3) that the interim termination of Doe's and all other Georgia pregnancies in existence in 1970 has not rendered the case moot; and (4) that Doe presents a justiciable controversy and has standing to maintain the action.

Inasmuch as Doe and her class are recognized, the question whether the other appellants—physicians, nurses, clergymen, social workers, and corporations—present a justiciable controversy and have standing is perhaps a matter of no great consequence. We conclude, however, that the physician-appellants, who are Georgia-licensed doctors consulted by pregnant women, also present a justiciable controversy and do have standing, despite the fact that the record does not disclose that any one of them has been prosecuted, or threatened with prosecution, for violation of the State's abortion statutes. The physician is the one against whom these criminal statutes directly operate in the event he procures an abortion that does not meet the statutory exceptions and conditions. The physician-appellants, therefore, assert a sufficiently direct threat of personal detriment. They should not be required to await and undergo a criminal prosecution as the sole means of seeking relief.

We distinguish this case from *Poe v. Ullman,* 367 U. S. 497 (1961). In that case, the challenged Connecticut statute, deemed to prohibit the giving of medical advice on the use of contraceptives, had been enacted in 1879, and, apparently with a single exception, no one had ever been prosecuted under it. Georgia's statute, in contrast, is recent and not moribund. Furthermore, it is the successor to another Georgia abortion statute under which, we are told,[9] physicians were prosecuted[. . . .]

The parallel claims of the nurse, clergy, social worker, and corporation-appellants are another step removed and as to them, the Georgia statutes operate less directly. Not being licensed physicians, the nurses and the others are in no position to render medical advice. They would be reached by the abortion statutes only in their capacity as accessories or as counselor-conspirators. We conclude that we need not pass upon the status of these additional appellants in this suit, for the issues are sufficiently and adequately presented by Doe and the physician-appellants, and nothing is gained or lost by the presence or absence of the nurses, the clergymen, the social workers, and the corporations. See *Roe v. Wade,* [page 13].

IV

The appellants attack on several grounds those portions of the Georgia abortion statutes that remain after the District Court decision: undue restriction of a right to personal and marital privacy;

[9] Tr[anscript] of Oral Arg. [pages] 21–22.

vagueness: deprivation of substantive and procedural due process; improper restriction to Georgia residents; and denial of equal protection.

A. *Roe v. Wade, supra,* sets forth our conclusion that a pregnant woman does not have an absolute constitutional right to an abortion on her demand. What is said there is applicable here and need not be repeated.

B. The appellants go on to argue, however, that the present Georgia statutes must be viewed historically, that is, from the fact that prior to the 1968 Act an abortion in Georgia was not criminal if performed to "preserve the life" of the mother. It is suggested that the present statute, as well, has this emphasis on the mother's rights, not on those of the fetus. Appellants contend that it is thus clear that Georgia has given little, and certainly not first, consideration to the unborn child. Yet, it is the unborn child's rights that Georgia asserts in justification of the statute. Appellants assert that this justification cannot be advanced at this late date.

Appellants then argue that the statutes do not adequately protect the woman's right. This is so because it would be physically and emotionally damaging to Doe to bring a child into her poor, "fatherless"[10] family, and because advances in medicine and medical techniques have made it safer for a woman to have a medically induced abortion than for her to bear a child. Thus, "a statute that requires a woman to carry an unwanted pregnancy to term infringes not only on a fundamental right of privacy but on the right to life itself." Brief 27.

The appellants recognize that a century ago medical knowledge was not so advanced as it is today, that the techniques of antisepsis were not known, and that any abortion procedure was dangerous for the woman. To restrict the legality of the abortion to the situation where it was deemed necessary, in medical judgment, for the preservation of the woman's life was only a natural conclusion in the exercise of the legislative judgment of that time. A State is not to be reproached, however, for a past judgmental determination made in the light of then-existing medical knowledge. It is perhaps unfair to argue, as the appellants do, that because the early focus was on the preservation of

---

[10] Brief for Appellants 25.

the woman's life, the State's present professed interest in the protection of embryonic and fetal life is to be downgraded. That argument denies the State the right to readjust its views and emphases in the light of the advanced knowledge and techniques of the day.

C. Appellants argue that § 26–1202 (a) of the Georgia statutes, as it has been left by the District Court's decision, is unconstitutionally vague. This argument centers on the proposition that, with the District Court's having struck down the statutorily specified reasons, it still remains a crime for a physician to perform an abortion except when, as § 26–1202 (a) reads, it is "based upon his best clinical judgment that an abortion is necessary." The appellants contend that the word "necessary" does not warn the physician of what conduct is proscribed; that the statute is wholly without objective standards and is subject to diverse interpretation; and that doctors will choose to err on the side of caution and will be arbitrary.

The net result of the District Court's decision is that the abortion determination, so far as the physician is concerned, is made in the exercise of his professional, that is, his "best clinical," judgment in the light of *all* the attendant circumstances. He is not now restricted to the three situations originally specified. Instead, he may range farther afield wherever his medical judgment, properly and professionally exercised, so dictates and directs him.

The vagueness argument is set at rest by the decision in *United States v. Vuitch*, 402 U. S. 62, 71-72 (1971), where the issue was raised with respect to a District of Columbia statute making abortions criminal "unless the same were done as necessary for the preservation of the mother's life or health and under the direction of a competent licensed practitioner of medicine." That statute has been construed to bear upon psychological as well as physical well-being. This being so, the Court concluded that the term "health" presented no problem of vagueness. "Indeed, whether a particular operation is necessary for a patient's physical or mental health is a judgment that physicians are obviously called upon to make routinely whenever surgery is considered." *Id.,* at 72. This conclusion is equally applicable here. Whether, in the words of the Georgia statute, "an abortion is necessary" is a professional judgment that the Georgia physician will be called upon to make routinely.

We agree with the District Court, 319 F. Supp., at 1058, that the medical judgment may be exercised in the light of all factors—physical, emotional, psychological, familial, and the woman's age—relevant to the well-being of the patient. All these factors may relate to health. This allows the attending physician the room he needs to make his best medical judgment. And it is room that operates for the benefit, not the disadvantage, of the pregnant woman.

D. The appellants next argue that the District Court should have declared unconstitutional three procedural demands of the Georgia statute: (1) that the abortion be performed in a hospital accredited by the Joint Commission on Accreditation of Hospitals:[11] (2) that the procedure be approved by the hospital staff abortion committee; and (3) that the performing physician's judgment be confirmed by the independent examinations of the patient by two other licensed physicians. The appellants attack these provisions not only on the ground that they unduly restrict the woman's right of privacy, but also on procedural due process and equal protection grounds. The physician-appellants also argue that, by subjecting a doctor's individual medical judgment to committee approval and to confirming consultations, the statute impermissibly restricts the physician's right to practice his profession and deprives him of due process.

1. JCAH accreditation. The Joint Commission on Accreditation of Hospitals is an organization without governmental sponsorship or overtones. No question whatever is raised concerning the integrity of the organization or the high purpose of the accreditation process.[12] That process, however, has to do with hospital standards generally and has no present particularized concern with abortion as a medical or surgical

---

[11] We were advised at reargument, Tr. of Oral Rearg. 10, that only 54 of Georgia's 159 counties have a JCAH-accredited hospital.

[12] Since its founding, JCAH has pursued the "elusive goal" of defining the "optimal setting" for "quality of service in hospitals." JCAH, Accreditation Manual for Hospitals, Foreword (Dec. 1970). The Manual's Introduction states the organization's purpose to establish standards and conduct accreditation programs that will afford quality medical care "to give patients the optimal benefits that medical science has to offer." This ambitious and admirable goal is illustrated by JCAH's decision in 1966 "[t]o raise and strengthen the standards from their present level of minimum essential to the level of optimum achievable...." Some of these "optimum achievable" standards required are: disclosure of hospital ownership and control; a dietetic service and written dietetic policies; a written disaster plan for mass emergencies; a nuclear medical services program; facilities for hematology, chemistry, microbiology, clinical microscopy, and sero-immunology; a professional library and document delivery service; a radiology program; a social services plan administered by a qualified social worker; and a special care unit.

procedure.[13] In Georgia, there is no restriction on the performance of non-abortion surgery in a hospital not yet accredited by the JCAH so long as other requirements imposed by the State, such as licensing of the hospital and of the operating surgeon, are met. See Georgia Code §§ 88–1901 (a) and 88–1905 (1971) and 84-907 (Supp. 1971). Furthermore, accreditation by the Commission is not granted until a hospital has been in operation at least one year. The Model Penal Code, § 230.3, Appendix B hereto, contains no requirement for JCAH accreditation. And the Uniform Abortion Act (Final Draft, Aug. 1971),[14] approved by the American Bar Association in February 1972, contains no JCAH-accredited hospital specification.[15] Some courts have held that a JCAH-accreditation requirement is an overbroad infringement of fundamental rights because it does not relate to the particular medical problems and dangers of the abortion operation. *E. g., Poe v. Menghini,* 339 F. Supp., at 993-994.

We hold that the JCAH-accreditation requirement does not withstand constitutional scrutiny in the present context. It is a requirement that simply is not "based on differences that are reasonably related to the purposes of the Act in which it is found." *Morey v. Doud,* 354 U. S. 457, 465 (1957).

This is not to say that Georgia may not or should not, from and after the end of the first trimester, adopt standards for licensing all facilities where abortions may be performed so long as those standards are legitimately related to the objective the State seeks to accomplish. The appellants contend that such a relationship would be lacking even in a lesser requirement that an abortion be performed in a licensed hospital, as opposed to a facility, such as a clinic, that may be required by the State to possess all the staffing and services necessary to perform an abortion safely (including those adequate to handle serious complications or other emergency, or arrangements with a nearby hospital to

[13] "The Joint Commission neither advocates nor opposes any particular position with respect to elective abortions." Letter dated July 9, 1971, from John I. Brewer, M. D., Commissioner, JCAH, to the Rockefeller Foundation. Brief for amici curiae, American College of Obstetricians and Gynecologists et al., p. A-3.

[14] [....]

[15] [.... Some states do not have the JCAH-accreditation requirement. Washington has the requirement, but couples it with the alternative of a "medical facility approved ... by the state board of health." Florida's new statute has a similar provision. The Delaware Code specifies a "nationally recognized medical or hospital accreditation authority."]

provide such services). Appellants and various *amici* have presented us with a mass of data purporting to demonstrate that some facilities other than hospitals are entirely adequate to perform abortions if they possess these qualifications. The State, on the other hand, has not presented persuasive data to show that only hospitals meet its acknowledged interest in insuring the quality of the operation and the full protection of the patient. We feel compelled to agree with appellants that the State must show more than it has in order to prove that only the full resources of a licensed hospital, rather than those of some other appropriately licensed institution, satisfy these health interests. We hold that the hospital requirement of the Georgia law, because it fails to exclude the first trimester of pregnancy, see *Roe v. Wade, ante,* at [p. 40], is also invalid. In so holding we naturally express no opinion on the medical judgment involved in any particular case, that is, whether the patient's situation is such that an abortion should be performed in a hospital, rather than in some other facility.

2. *Committee approval.* The second aspect of the appellants' procedural attack relates to the hospital abortion committee and to the pregnant woman's asserted lack of access to that committee. Relying primarily on *Goldberg v. Kelly,* 397 U. S. 254 (1970), concerning the termination of welfare benefits, and *Wisconsin v. Constantineau,* 400 U. S. 433 (1971), concerning the posting of an alcoholic's name, Doe first argues that she was denied due process because she could not make a presentation to the committee. It is not clear from the record, however, whether Doe's own consulting physician was or was not a member of the committee or did or did not present her case, or, indeed, whether she herself was or was not there. We see nothing in the Georgia statute that explicitly denies access to the committee by or on behalf of the woman. If the access point alone were involved, we would not be persuaded to strike down the committee provision on the unsupported assumption that access is not provided.

Appellants attack the discretion the statute leaves to the committee. The most concrete argument they advance is their suggestion that it is still a badge of infamy "in many minds" to bear an illegitimate child, and that the Georgia system enables the committee members' personal views as to extramarital sex relations, and punishment therefor, to govern their decisions. This approach obviously is one founded on suspicion and one that discloses a lack of confidence in the integrity of physicians. To say that physicians will be guided in their hospital committee decisions by their predilections on extramarital sex unduly narrows the issue to pregnancy outside marriage. (Doe's own situation did not involve extramarital sex and its product.) The appellants' suggestion is necessarily somewhat degrading to the conscientious physician, particularly the obstetrician, whose professional activity is concerned with the physical and mental welfare, the woes, the emotions, and the concern of his female patients. He, perhaps more than anyone else, is knowledgeable in this area of patient care, and he is aware of human frailty, so-called "error," and needs. The good physician—despite the presence of rascals in the medical profession, as in all others, we trust that most physicians are "good"—will have sympathy and understanding for the pregnant patient that probably are not exceeded by those who participate in other areas of professional counseling.

It is perhaps worth noting that the abortion committee has a function of its own. It is a committee of the hospital and it is composed of members of the institution's medical staff. The membership usually is a changing one. In this way, its work burden is shared and is more readily accepted. The committee's function is protective. It enables the hospital appropriately to be advised that its posture and activities are in accord with legal requirements. It is to be remembered that the hospital is an entity and that it, too, has legal rights and legal obligations.

Saying all this, however, does not settle the issue of the constitutional propriety of the committee requirement. Viewing the Georgia statute as a whole, we see no constitutionally justifiable pertinence in the structure for the advance approval by the abortion committee. With regard to the protection of potential life, the medical judgment is already completed prior to the committee stage, and review by a committee once removed from diagnosis is basically redundant. We are not cited to any other surgical procedure made subject to committee approval as a matter of state criminal law. The woman's right to receive medical care in accordance with her licensed physician's best judgment and the physician's right to administer it are substantially limited by this statutorily imposed overview. And the hospital itself is otherwise fully protected. Under § 26–1202 (e), the hospital is free not to admit a patient for an abortion. It is even free not to have an abortion committee. Further, a physician or any other employee has the right to refrain, for moral or religious reasons, from participating in the abortion procedure. These provisions obviously are in the statute in order to afford appropriate protection to the individual and to the denominational hospital. Section 26–1202 (e) affords adequate protection to the hospital, and little more is provided by the committee prescribed by § 26–1202 (b) (5).

We conclude that the interposition of the hospital abortion committee is unduly restrictive of the patient's rights and needs that, at this point, have already been medically delineated and substantiated by her personal physician. To ask more serves neither the hospital nor the State.

3. *Two-doctor concurrence.* The third aspect of the appellants' attack centers on the "time and availability of adequate medical facilities and personnel." It is said that the system imposes substantial and irrational roadblocks and "is patently unsuited" to prompt determination of the abortion decision. Time, of course, is critical in abortion. Risks during the first trimester of pregnancy are admittedly lower than during later months.

The appellants purport to show by a local study[16] of Grady Memorial Hospital (serving indigent residents in Fulton and DeKalb Counties) that the "mechanics of the system itself forced . . . discontinuance of the abortion process" because the median time for the workup was 15 days. The same study shows, however, that 27% of the candidates for abortion were already 13 or more weeks pregnant at the time of application, that is, they were at the end of or beyond the first trimester when they made their applications. It is too much to say, as appellants do, that these particular persons "were victims of a system over which they [had] no control." If higher risk was incurred because of abortions in the second rather than the first trimester, much of that risk was due to delay in application, and not to the alleged cumbersomeness of the system. We note, in passing, that appellant Doe had no delay problem herself; the decision in her case was made well within the first trimester.

---

[16] [. . . .]

It should be manifest that our rejection of the accredited-hospital requirement and, more important, of the abortion committee's advance approval eliminates the major grounds of the attack based on the system's delay and the lack of facilities. There remains, however, the required confirmation by two Georgia-licensed physicians in addition to the recommendation of the pregnant woman's own consultant (making under the statute, a total of six physicians involved, including the three on the hospital's abortion committee). We conclude that this provision, too, must fall.

The statute's emphasis, as has been repetitively noted, is on the attending physician's "best clinical judgment that an abortion is necessary." That should be sufficient. The reasons for the presence of the confirmation step in the statute are perhaps apparent, but they are insufficient to withstand constitutional challenge. Again, no other voluntary medical or surgical procedure for which Georgia requires confirmation by two other physicians has been cited to us. If a physician is licensed by the State, he is recognized by the State as capable of exercising acceptable clinical judgment. If he fails in this, professional censure and deprivation of his license are available remedies. Required acquiescence by co-practitioners has no rational connection with a patient's needs and unduly infringes on the physician's right to practice. The attending physician will know when a consultation is advisable—the doubtful situation, the need for assurance when the medical decision is a delicate one, and the like. Physicians have followed this routine historically and know its usefulness and benefit for all concerned. It is still true today that "[r]eliance must be placed upon the assurance given by his license, issued by an authority competent to judge in that respect, that he [the physician] possesses the requisite qualifications." *Dent v. West Virginia,* 129 U. S. 114, 122–123 (1889). See *United States v. Vuitch,* 402 U. S., at 71.

E. The appellants attack the residency requirement of the Georgia law, §§ 26–1202 (b) (1) and (b) (2), as violative of the right to travel stressed in *Shapiro v. Thompson,* 394 U. S. 618, 629–631 (1969), and other cases. A requirement of this kind, of course, could be deemed to have some relationship to the availability of post-procedure medical care for the aborted patient.

Nevertheless, we do not uphold the constitutionality of the

residence requirement. It is not based on any policy of preserving state-supported facilities for Georgia residents, for the bar also applies to private hospitals and to privately retained physicians. There is no intimation, either, that Georgia facilities are utilized to capacity in caring for Georgia residents. Just as the Privileges and Immunities Clause, Const. Art. IV, § 2, protects persons who enter other States to ply their trade, *Ward v. Maryland,* 12 Wall. 418, 430 (1871); *Blake v. McClung,* 172 U. S. 239, 248–256 (1898), so must it protect persons who enter Georgia seeking the medical services that are available there. See *Toomer v. Witsell,* 334 U. S. 385, 396–397 (1948). A contrary holding would mean that a State could limit to its own residents the general medical care available within its borders. This we could not approve.

F. The last argument on this phase of the case is one that often is made, namely, that the Georgia system is violative of equal protection because it discriminates against the poor. The appellants do not urge that abortions should be performed by persons other than licensed physicians, so we have no argument that because the wealthy can better afford physicians, the poor should have non-physicians made available to them. The appellants acknowledged that the procedures are "nondiscriminatory in ... express terms" but they suggest that they have produced invidious discriminations. The District Court rejected this approach out of hand. 319 F. Supp., at 1056. It rests primarily on the accreditation and approval and confirmation requirements, discussed above, and on the assertion that most of Georgia's counties have no accredited hospital. We have set aside the accreditation, approval, and confirmation requirements, however, and with that, the discrimination argument collapses in all significant aspects.

V

The appellants complain, finally, of the District Court's denial of injunctive relief. A like claim was made in *Roe v. Wade,* [p. 13]. We declined decision there insofar as injunctive relief was concerned, and we decline it here. We assume that Georgia's prosecutorial authorities will give full recognition to the judgment of this Court.

In summary, we hold that the JCAH-accredited hospital provision and the requirements as to approval by the hospital abortion committee, as to confirmation by two independent physicians, and as to residence in Georgia are all violative of the Fourteenth Amendment. Specifically, the following portions of § 26–1202 (b), remaining after the District Court's judgment, are invalid:

(1) Subsections (1) and (2).

(2) That portion of Subsection (3) following the words "[s]uch physician's judgment is reduced to writing."

(3) Subsections (4) and (5).

The judgment of the District Court is modified accordingly and, as so modified, is affirmed. Costs are allowed to the appellants.

MR. CHIEF JUSTICE BURGER, concurring*.

I agree that, under the Fourteenth Amendment to the Constitution, the abortion statutes of Georgia and Texas impermissibly limit the performance of abortions necessary to protect the health of pregnant women, using the term health in its broadest medical context. See *United States v. Vuitch*, 402 U. S. 62, 71–72 (1971). I am somewhat troubled that the Court has taken notice of various scientific and medical data in reaching its conclusion; however, I do not believe that the Court has exceeded the scope of judicial notice accepted in other contexts.

In oral argument, counsel for the State of Texas informed the Court that early abortion procedures were routinely permitted in certain exceptional cases, such as nonconsensual pregnancies resulting from rape and incest. In the face of a rigid and narrow statute, such as that of Texas, no one in these circumstances should be placed in a posture of dependence on a prosecutorial policy or prosecutorial discretion. Of course, States must have broad power, within the limits indicated in the opinions, to regulate the subject of abortions, but where the consequences of state intervention are so severe, uncertainty must be avoided as much as possible. For my part, I would be inclined to allow a State to require the certification of two physicians to support an abortion, but the Court holds otherwise. I do not believe that such a procedure is unduly burdensome, as are the complex steps of the Georgia statute, which require as many as six doctors and the use of a hospital certified by the JCAH.

I do not read the Court's holdings today as having the sweeping consequences attributed to them by the dissenting Justices; the dissenting views discount the reality that the vast majority of physicians observe the standards of their profession, and act only on the basis of carefully deliberated medical judgments relating to life and health. Plainly, the Court today rejects any claim that the Constitution requires abortions on demand.

---

*[This opinion applies also to No. 70–18, *Roe v. Wade*.]

MR. JUSTICE DOUGLAS, concurring*

While I join the opinion of the Court,[1] I add a few words.

I

The questions presented in the present cases go far beyond the issues of vagueness, which we considered in *United States v. Vuitch,* 402 U. S. 62. They involve the right of privacy, one aspect of which we considered in *Griswold v. Connecticut,* 381 U. S. 479, 484, when we held that various guarantees in the Bill of Rights create zones of privacy.[2]

The *Griswold* case involved a law forbidding the use of contraceptives. We held that law as applied to married people unconstitutional:

> "We deal with a right of privacy older than the Bill of Rights—older than our political parties, older than our school system. Marriage is a coming together for better or for worse, hopefully enduring, and intimate to the degree of being sacred." *Id.,* at 486.

The District Court in *Doe* held that *Griswold* and related cases

---

*This opinion applies also to No. 70–18, Roe v. Wade.

[1] I disagree with the dismissal of Dr. Hallford's complaint, in intervention in *Roe v. Wade, ante,* p. 113, because my disagreement with *Younger v. Harris,* 401 U. S. 37, revealed in my dissent in that case, still persists and extends to the progeny of that case.

[2] There is no mention of privacy in our Bill of Rights but our decisions have recognized it as one of the fundamental values those amendments were designed to protect. The fountainhead case is *Boyd v. United States,* 116 U. S. 616, holding that a federal statute which authorized a court in tax cases to require a taxpayer to produce his records or to concede the Government's allegations offended the Fourth and Fifth Amendments. Mr. Justice Bradley, for the Court, found that the measure unduly intruded into the "sanctity of a man's home and the privacies of life." *Id.,* at 630. Prior to *Boyd,* in *Kilbourn v. Thompson,* 103 U. S. 168, 190, Mr. Justice Miller held for the Court that neither House of Congress "possesses the general power of making inquiry into the private affairs of the citizen." Of *Kilbourn,* Mr. Justice Field later said, "This case will stand for all time as a bulwark against the invasion of the right of the citizen to protection in his private affairs against the unlimited scrutiny of investigation by a congressional committee." *In re Pacific Railway Comm'n,* 32 F. 241, 253 (cited with approval in *Sinclair v. United States,* 279 U. S. 263, 293). Mr. Justice Harlan, also speaking for the Court, in *ICC v. Brimson,* 154 U. S. 447, 478, thought the same was true of administrative inquiries, saying that the Constitution did not permit a "general power of making inquiry into the private affairs of the citizen." In a similar vein were *Harriman v. ICC,* 211 U. S. 407; *United States v. Louisville & Nashville R. Co.,* 236 U. S. 318, 335; and *FTC v. American Tobacco Co.,* 264 U. S. 298.

"establish a Constitutional right to privacy broad enough to encompass the right of a woman to terminate an unwanted pregnancy in its early stages, by obtaining an abortion." 319 F. Supp. 1048, 1054.

The Supreme Court of California expressed the same view in *People v. Belous*,[3] 71 Cal. 2d 954, 963, 458 P. 2d 194, 199.

The Ninth Amendment obviously does not create federally pass enforceable rights. It merely says, "The enumeration in the Constitution, of certain rights, shall not be construed to deny or disparage others retained by the people." But a catalogue of these rights includes customary, traditional, and time-honored rights, amenities, privileges, and immunities that come within the sweep of "the Blessings of Liberty" mentioned in the preamble to the Constitution. Many of them, in my view, come within the meaning of the term "liberty" as used in the Fourteenth Amendment.

First is the autonomous control over the development and expression of one's intellect, interests, tastes, and personality.

These are rights protected by the First Amendment and, in my view, they are absolute, permitting of no exceptions. See *Terminiello v. Chicago*, 337 U. S. 1; *Roth v. United States*, 354 U. S. 476, 508 (dissent); *Kingsley Pictures Corp. v. Regents*, 360 U. S. 684, 697 (concurring); *New York Times Co. v. Sullivan*, 376 U. S. 254, 293 (Black, J., concurring, in which I joined). The Free Exercise Clause of the First Amendment is one facet of this constitutional right. The right to remain silent as respects one's own beliefs, *Watkins v. United States*, 354 U. S. 178, 196–199, is protected by the First and the Fifth. The First Amendment grants the privacy of first-class mail, *United States v. Van Leeuwen*, 397 U. S. 249, 253. All of these aspects of the right of privacy are rights "retained by the people" in the meaning of the Ninth Amendment.

Second is freedom of choice in the basic decisions of one's life respecting marriage, divorce, procreation, contraception, and the education and upbringing of children.

These rights, unlike those protected by the First Amendment, are subject to some control by the police power. Thus, the Fourth Amendment speaks only of "unreasonable searches and seizures" and

---

[3] The California abortion statute, held unconstitutional in the *Belous* case, made it a crime to perform or help perform an abortion "unless the same is necessary to preserve [the mother's] life." 71 Cal. 2d, at 959, 458 P. 2d, at 197.

of "probable cause." These rights are "fundamental," and we have held that in order to support legislative action the statute must be narrowly and precisely drawn and that a "compelling state interest" must be shown in support of the limitation. *E. g., Kramer v. Union Free School District,* 395 U. S. 621; *Shapiro v. Thompson,* 394 U. S. 618; *Carrington v. Rash,* 380 U. S. 89; *Sherbert v. Verner,* 374 U. S. 398; *NAACP v. Alabama,* 357 U. S. 449.

The liberty to marry a person of one's own choosing, *Loving v. Virginia,* 388 U. S. 1; the right of procreation, *Skinner v. Oklahoma,* 316 U. S. 535; the liberty to direct the education of one's children, *Pierce v. Society of Sisters,* 268 U. S. 510, and the privacy of the marital relation, *Griswold v. Connecticut, supra,* are in this category.[4] Only last Term in *Eisenstadt v. Baird,* 405 U. S. 438, another contraceptive case, we expanded the concept of *Griswold* by saying:

"It is true in *Griswold* the right of privacy in question inhered in the marital relationship. Yet the marital couple is not an independent entity with a mind and heart of its own, but an association of two individuals each with a separate intellectual and emotional makeup. If the right of privacy means anything, it is the right of the *individual,* married or single, to be free from unwarranted governmental intrusion into matters so funda-

---

[4] My Brother STEWART, writing in *Roe v. Wade, supra,* says that our decision in *Griswold* reintroduced substantive due process that had been rejected in *Ferguson v. Skrupa,* 372 U. S. 726. *Skrupa* involved legislation governing a business enterprise; and the Court in that case, as had Mr. Justice Holmes on earlier occasions, rejected the idea that "liberty" within the meaning of the Due Process Clause of the Fourteenth Amendment was a vessel to be filled with one's personal choices of values, whether drawn from the *laissez faire* school, from the socialistic school, or from the technocrats. *Griswold* involved legislation touching on the marital relation and involving the conviction of a licensed physician for giving married people information concerning contraception. There is nothing specific in the Bill of Rights that covers that item. Nor is there anything in the Bill of Rights that in terms protects the right of association or the privacy in one's association. Yet we found those rights in the periphery of the First Amendment. *NAACP v. Alabama,* 357 U. S. 449, 462. Other peripheral rights are the right to educate one's children as one chooses, *Pierce v. Society of Sisters,* 268 U. S. 510, and the right to study the German language, *Meyer v. Nebraska,* 262 U. S. 390. These decisions, with all respect, have nothing to do with substantive due process. One may think they are not peripheral to other rights that are expressed in the Bill of Rights. But that is not enough to bring into play the protection of substantive due process.

There are, of course, those who have believed that the reach of due process in the Fourteenth Amendment included all of the Bill of Rights but went further. Such was the view of Mr. Justice Murphy and Mr. Justice Rutledge. See *Adamson v. California,* 332 U. S. 46, 123, 124 (dissenting opinion). Perhaps they were right; but it is a bridge that neither I nor those who joined the Court's opinion in *Griswold* crossed.

mentally affecting a person as the decision whether to bear or beget a child." *Id.*, at 453.

This right of privacy was called by Mr. Justice Brandeis the right "to be let alone." *Olmstead v. United States,* 277 U. S. 438, 478 (dissenting opinion). That right includes the privilege of an individual to plan his own affairs, for "'outside areas of plainly harmful conduct, every American is left to shape his own life as he thinks best, do what he pleases, go where he pleases.'" *Kent v. Dulles,* 357 U. S. 116, 126.

Third is the freedom to care for one's health and person, freedom from bodily restraint or compulsion, freedom to walk, stroll, or loaf.

These rights, though fundamental, are likewise subject to regulation on a showing of "compelling state interest." We stated in *Papachristou v. City of Jacksonville,* 405 U. S. 156, 164, that walking, strolling, and wandering "are historically part of the amenities of life as we have known them." As stated in *Jacobson v. Massachusetts,* 197 U. S. 11, 29:

> "There is, of course, a sphere within which the individual may assert the supremacy of his own will and rightfully dispute the authority of any human government, especially of any free government existing under a written constitution, to interfere with the exercise of that will."

In *Union Pacific R. Co. v Botsford,* 141 U. S. 250, 252, the Court said, "The inviolability of the person is as much invaded by a compulsory stripping and exposure as by a blow."

In *Terry v. Ohio,* 392 U. S. 1, 8-9, the Court, in speaking of the Fourth Amendment stated, "This inestimable right of personal security belongs as much to the citizen on the streets of our cities as to the homeowner closeted in his study to dispose of his secret affairs."

Katz v. United States, 389 U. S. 347, 350, emphasizes that the Fourth Amendment "protects individual privacy against certain kinds of governmental intrusion."

In *Meyer v. Nebraska,* 262 U. S. 390, 399, the Court said:

> "Without doubt, [liberty] denotes not merely freedom from bodily restraint but also the right of the individual to contract, to engage in any of the common occupations of life, to acquire useful knowledge, to marry, establish a home and bring up children, to worship God according to the dictates of his own

conscience, and generally to enjoy those privileges long recognized at common law as essential to the orderly pursuit of happiness by free men."

The Georgia statute is at war with the clear message of these cases—that a woman is free to make the basic decision whether to bear an unwanted child. Elaborate argument is hardly necessary to demonstrate that childbirth may deprive a woman of her preferred lifestyle and force upon her a radically different and undesired future. For example, rejected applicants under the Georgia statute are required to endure the discomforts of pregnancy; to incur the pain, higher mortality rate, and aftereffects of childbirth; to abandon educational plans; to sustain loss of income; to forgo the satisfactions of careers; to tax further mental and physical health in providing child care; and, in some cases, to bear the lifelong stigma of unwed motherhood, a badge which may haunt, if not deter, later legitimate family relationships.

II

Such reasoning is, however, only the beginning of the problem. The State has interests to protect. Vaccinations to prevent epidemics are one example, as *Jacobson, supra,* holds. The Court held that compulsory sterilization of imbeciles afflicted with hereditary forms of insanity or imbecility is another. *Buck v. Bell,* 274 U. S. 200. Abortion affects another. While childbirth endangers the lives of some women, voluntary abortion at any time and place regardless of medical standards would impinge on a rightful concern of society. The woman's health is part of that concern; as is the life of the fetus after quickening. These concerns justify the State in treating the procedure as a medical one.

One difficulty is that this statute as construed and applied apparently does not give full sweep to the "psychological as well as physical well-being" of women patients which saved the concept "health" from being void for vagueness in *United States v. Vuitch,* 402 U. S., at 72. But, apart from that, Georgia's enactment has a constitutional infirmity because, as stated by the District Court, it "limits the number of reasons for which an abortion may be sought." I agree with the holding of the District Court, "This the State may not do, because such action unduly restricts a decision sheltered by the

Constitutional right to privacy." 319 F. Supp., at 1056.

The vicissitudes of life produce pregnancies which may be unwanted, or which may impair "health" in the broad *Vuitch* sense of the term, or which may imperil the life of the mother, or which in the full setting of the case may create such suffering, dislocations, misery, or tragedy as to make an early abortion the only civilized step to take. These hardships may be properly embraced in the "health" factor of the mother as appraised by a person of insight. Or they may be part of a broader medical judgment based on what is "appropriate" in a given case, though perhaps not "necessary" in a strict sense.

The "liberty" of the mother, though rooted as it is in the Constitution, may be qualified by the State for the reasons we have stated. But where fundamental personal rights and liberties are involved, the corrective legislation must be "narrowly drawn to prevent the supposed evil," *Cantwell v. Connecticut,* 310 U. S. 296, 307, and not be dealt with in an "unlimited and indiscriminate" manner. *Shelton v. Tucker,* 364 U. S. 479, 490. And see *Talley v. California,* 362 U. S. 60. Unless regulatory measures are so confined and are addressed to the specific areas of compelling legislative concern, the police power would become the great leveler of constitutional rights and liberties.

There is no doubt that the State may require abortions to be performed by qualified medical personnel. The legitimate objective of preserving the mother's health clearly supports such laws. Their impact upon the woman's privacy is minimal. But the Georgia statute outlaws virtually all such operations—even in the earliest stages of pregnancy. The light of modern medical evidence suggesting that an early abortion is safer healthwise than childbirth itself,[5] it cannot be seriously urged that so comprehensive a ban is aimed at protecting the woman's health. Rather, this expansive proscription of all abortions along the temporal spectrum can rest only on a public goal of preserving both embryonic and fetal life.

The present statute has struck the balance between the woman's

---

[5] Many studies show that it is safer for a woman to have a medically induced abortion than to bear a child. In the first 11 months of operation of the New York abortion law, the mortality rate associated with such operations was six per 100,000 operations. [. . . .] On the other hand, the maternal mortality rate associated with childbirths other than abortions was 18 per 100,000 live births. [. . . .]

and the State's interests wholly in favor of the latter. I am not prepared to hold that a State may equate, as Georgia has done, all phases of maturation preceding birth. We held in *Griswold* that the States may not preclude spouses from attempting to avoid the joinder of sperm and egg. If this is true, it is difficult to perceive any overriding public necessity which might attach precisely at the moment of conception. As Mr. Justice Clark has said:[6]

> "To say that life is present at conception is to give recognition to the potential, rather than the actual. The unfertilized egg has life, and if fertilized, it takes on human proportions. But the law deals in reality, not obscurity—the known rather than the unknown. When sperm meets egg life may eventually form, but quite often it does not. The law does not deal in speculation. The phenomenon of life takes time to develop, and until it is actually present, it cannot be destroyed. Its interruption prior to formation would hardly be homicide, and as we have seen, society does not regard it as such. The rites of Baptism are not performed and death certificates are not required when a miscarriage occurs. No prosecutor has ever returned a murder indictment charging the taking of the life of a fetus.[7] This would not be the case if the fetus constituted human life."

In summary, the enactment is overbroad. It is not closely correlated to the aim of preserving prenatal life. In fact, it permits its destruction in several cases, including pregnancies resulting from sex acts in which unmarried females are below the statutory age of consent. At the same time, however, the measure broadly proscribes aborting other pregnancies which may cause severe mental disorders. Additionally, the statute is overbroad because it equates the value of embryonic life immediately after conception with the worth of life immediately before birth.

---

[6] [....]

[7] In *Keeler v. Superior Court*, 2 Cal. 3d 619, 470 P. 2d 617, the California Supreme Court held in 1970 that the California murder statute did not cover the killing of an unborn fetus, even though the fetus be "viable," and that it was beyond judicial power to extend the statute to the killing of an unborn. It held that the child must be "born alive before a charge of homicide can be sustained." *Id.*, at 639, 470 P. 2d, at 630.

III

Under the Georgia Act, the mother's physician is not the sole judge as to whether the abortion should be performed. Two other licensed physicians must concur in his judgment.[8] Moreover, the abortion must be performed in a licensed hospital;[9] and the abortion must be approved in advance by a committee of the medical staff of that hospital.[10]

Physicians, who speak to us in *Doe* through an *amicus* brief, complain of the Georgia Act's interference with their practice of their profession.

The right of privacy has no more conspicuous place than in the physician-patient relationship, unless it be in the priest-penitent relationship.

It is one thing for a patient to agree that her physician may consult with another physician about her case. It is quite a different matter for the State compulsorily to impose on that physician-patient relationship another layer or, as in this case, still a third layer of physicians. The right of privacy—the right to care for one's health and person and to seek out a physician of one's own choice protected by the Fourteenth Amendment—becomes only a matter of theory, not a reality, when a multiple-physician-approval system is mandated by the State.

The State licenses a physician. If he is derelict or faithless, the procedures available to punish him or to deprive him of his license are well known. He is entitled to procedural due process before professional disciplinary sanctions may be imposed. See *In re Ruffalo,* 390 U. S. 544. Crucial here, however, is state-imposed control over the medical decision whether pregnancy should be interrupted. The good-faith decision of the patient's chosen physician is overridden and the final decision passed on to others in whose selection the patient has no part. This is a total destruction of the right of privacy between physician and patient and the intimacy of relation which that entails.

The right to seek advice on one's health and the right to place reliance on the physician of one's choice are basic to Fourteenth Amendment values. We deal with fundamental rights and liberties,

8, 9, 10 [. . . .]

which, as already noted, can be contained or controlled only be discretely drawn legislation that preserves the "liberty" and regulates only those phases of the problem of compelling legislative concern. The imposition by the State of group controls over the physician-patient relationship is not made on any medical procedure apart from abortion, no matter how dangerous the medical step may be. The oversight imposed on the physician and patient in abortion cases denies them their "liberty," *viz.*, their right of privacy, without any compelling, discernible state interest.

Georgia has constitutional warrant in treating abortion as a medical problem. To protect the woman's right of privacy, however, the control must be through the physician of her choice and the standards set for his performance.

The protection of the fetus when it has acquired life is a legitimate concern of the State. Georgia's law makes no rational, discernible decision on that score.[11] For under the Code, the developmental stage of the fetus is irrelevant when pregnancy is the result of rape, when the fetus will very likely be born with a permanent defect, or when a continuation of the pregnancy will endanger the life of the mother or permanently injure her health. When life is present is a question we do not try to resolve. While basically a question for medical experts, as stated by Mr. Justice Clark,[12] it is, of course, caught up in matters of religion and morality.

In short, I agree with the Court that endangering the life of the woman or seriously and permanently injuring her health are standards too narrow for the right of privacy that is at stake.

I also agree that the superstructure of medical supervision which Georgia has erected violates the patient's right of privacy inherent in her choice of her own physician.

Mr. Justice White, with whom Mr. Justice Rehnquist joins, dissenting.*

At the heart of the controversy in these cases are those recurring pregnancies that pose no danger whatsoever to the life or health of the

---

[11, 12] [. . . .]

* [This opinion applies also to No. 70–18, *Roe v. Wade, ante,* p. 13.]

mother but are, nevertheless, unwanted for any one or more of a variety of reasons—convenience, family planning, economics, dislike of children, the embarrassment of illegitimacy, etc. The common claim before us is that for any one of such reasons, or for no reason at all, and without asserting or claiming any threat to life or health, any woman is entitled to an abortion at her request if she is able to find a medical advisor willing to undertake the procedure.

The Court for the most part sustains this position: During the period prior to the time the fetus becomes viable, the Constitution of the United States values the convenience, whim, or caprice of the putative mother more than the life or potential life of the fetus; the Constitution, therefore, guarantees the right to an abortion as against any state law or policy seeking to protect the fetus from an abortion not prompted by more compelling reasons of the mother.

With all due respect, I dissent. I find nothing in the language or history of the Constitution to support the Court's judgment. The Court simply fashions and announces a new constitutional right for pregnant mothers and, with scarcely any reason or authority for its action, invests that right with sufficient substance to override most existing state abortion statutes. The upshot is that the people and the legislatures of the 50 States are constitutionally disentitled to weigh the relative importance of the continued existence and development of the fetus, on the one hand, against a spectrum of possible impacts on the mother, on the other hand. As an exercise of raw judicial power, the Court perhaps has authority to do what it does today; but in my view its judgment is an improvident and extravagant exercise of the power of judicial review that the Constitution extends to this Court.

The Court apparently values the convenience of the pregnant mother more than the continued existence and development of the life or potential life that she carries. Whether or not I might agree with that marshaling of values, I can in no event join the Court's judgment because I find no constitutional warrant for imposing such an order of priorities on the people and legislatures of the States. In a sensitive area such as this, involving as it does issues over which reasonable men may easily and heatedly differ, I cannot accept the Court's exercise of its clear power of choice by interposing a constitutional barrier to state efforts to protect human life and by investing mothers and doctors with the constitutionally protected right to exterminate it. This issue, for the most part, should be left with the people and to the political processes the people have devised to govern their affairs.

It is my view, therefore, that the Texas statute is not constitutionally infirm because it denies abortions to those who seek to serve only their convenience rather than to protect their life or health. Nor is this plaintiff, who claims no threat to her mental or physical health, entitled to assert the possible rights of those women whose pregnancy assertedly implicates their health. This, together with *United States v. Vuitch,* 402 U. S. 62 (1971), dictates reversal of the judgment of the District Court.

Likewise, because Georgia may constitutionally forbid abortions to putative mothers who, like the plaintiff in this case, do not fall within the reach of § 26–1202 (a) of its criminal code, I have no occasion, and the District Court had none, to consider the constitutionality of the procedural requirements of the Georgia statute as applied to those pregnancies posing substantial hazards to either life or health. I would reverse the judgment of the District Court in the Georgia case.

MR. JUSTICE REHNQUIST, dissenting.

The holding in *Roe v. Wade* [page 13], that state abortion laws can withstand constitutional scrutiny only if the State can demonstrate a compelling state interest, apparently compels the Court's close scrutiny of the various provisions in Georgia's abortion statute. Since, as indicated by my dissent in *Wade,* I view the compelling-state-interest standard as an inappropriate measure of the constitutionality of state abortion laws, I respectfully dissent from the majority's holding.

APPENDIX A TO OPINION OF THE COURT

[This Appendix accompanies the majority decision.]

Criminal Code of Georgia

(The italicized portions are those held unconstitutional by the District Court)

CHAPTER 26–12. ABORTION.

26–1201. Criminal Abortion. Except as otherwise provided in section 26–1202, a person commits criminal abortion when he administers any medicine, drug or other substance whatever to any woman or when he uses any instrument or other means whatever upon any woman with intent to produce a miscarriage or abortion.

26–1202. Exception. (a) Section 26–1201 shall not apply to an abortion performed by a physician duly licensed to practice medicine and surgery pursuant to Chapter 84-9 or 84-12 of the Code of Georgia of 1933, as amended, based upon his best clinical judgment that an abortion is necessary because:

(1) A continuation of the pregnancy would endanger the life of the pregnant woman or would seriously and permanently injure her health; or

(2) The fetus would very likely be born with a grave, permanent, and irremediable mental or physical defect; or

(3) The pregnancy resulted from forcible or statutory rape.

(b) No abortion is authorized or shall be performed under this section unless each of the following conditions is met:

(1) The pregnant woman requesting the abortion certifies in writing under oath and subject to the penalties of false swearing to the physician who proposes to perform the abortion that she is a bona fide legal resident of the State of Georgia.

(2) The physician certifies that he believes the woman is a bona fide resident of this State and that he has no information which should lead him to believe otherwise.

(3) Such physician's judgment is reduced to writing and concurred in by at least two other physicians duly licensed to practice medicine and surgery pursuant to Chapter 84-9 of the Code of Georgia of 1933, as amended, who certify in writing that based upon

their separate personal medical examinations of the pregnant woman, the abortion is, in their judgment, necessary *because of one or more of the reasons enumerated above.*

(4) Such abortion is performed in a hospital licensed by the State Board of Health and accredited by the Joint Commission on Accreditation of Hospitals.

(5) The performance of the abortion has been approved in advance by a committee of the medical staff of the hospital in which the operation is to be performed. This committee must be one established and maintained in accordance with the standards promulgated by the Joint Commission on the Accreditation of Hospitals, and its approval must be by a majority vote of a membership of not less than three members of the hospital's staff; the physician proposing to perform the operation may not be counted as a member of the committee for this purpose.

(6) If the proposed abortion is considered necessary because the woman has been raped, the woman makes a written statement under oath, and subject to the penalties of false swearing, of the date, time and place of the rape and the name of the rapist, if known. There must be attached to this statement a certified copy of any report of the rape made by any law enforcement officer or agency and a statement by the solicitor general of the judicial circuit where the rape occurred or allegedly occurred that, according to his best information, there is probable cause to believe that the rape did occur.

(7) Such written opinions, statements, certificates, and concurrences are maintained in the permanent files of such hospital and are available at all reasonable times to the solicitor general of the judicial circuit in which the hospital is located.

(8) A copy of such written opinions, statements, certificates, and concurrences is filed with the Director of the State Department of Public Health within 10 days after such operation is performed.

(9) All written opinions, statements, certificates, and concurrences filed and maintained pursuant to paragraphs (7) and (8) of this subsection shall be confidential records and shall not be made available for public inspection at any time.

(c) Any solicitor general of the judicial circuit in which an abortion is to be performed under this section, or any person who would be a relative

of the child within the second degree of consanguinity, may petition the superior court of the county in which the abortion is to be performed for a declaratory judgment whether the performance of such abortion would violate any constitutional or other legal rights of the fetus. Such solicitor general may also petition such court for the purpose of taking issue with compliance with the requirements of this section. The physician who proposes to perform the abortion and the pregnant woman shall be respondents. The petition shall be heard expeditiously and if the court adjudges that such abortion would violate the constitutional or other legal rights of the fetus, the court shall so declare and shall restrain the physician from performing the abortion.

(d) If an abortion is performed in compliance with this section, the death of the fetus shall not give rise to any claim for wrongful death.

(e) Nothing in this section shall require a hospital to admit any patient under the provisions hereof for the purpose of performing an abortion, nor shall any hospital be required to appoint a committee such as contemplated under subsection (b) (5). A physician, or any other person who is a member of or associated with the staff of a hospital, or any employee of a hospital in which an abortion has been authorized, who shall state in writing an objection to such abortion on moral or religious grounds shall not be required to participate in the medical procedures which will result in the abortion, and the refusal of any such person to participate therein shall not form the basis of any claim for damages on account of such refusal or for any disciplinary or recriminatory action against such person.

26–1203. Punishment. A person convicted of criminal abortion shall be punished by imprisonment for not less than one nor more than 10 years.

APPENDIX B TO OPINION OF THE COURT
[This Appendix accompanies the majority decision.]

American Law Institute

MODEL PENAL CODE

Section 230.3. Abortion

(1) *Unjustified Abortion.* A person who purposely and unjustifiably terminates the pregnancy of another otherwise than by a live birth commits a felony of the third degree or, where the pregnancy has continued beyond the twenty-sixth week, a felony of the second degree.

(2) *Justifiable Abortion.* A licensed physician is justified in terminating a pregnancy if he believes there is substantial risk that continuance of the pregnancy would gravely impair the physical or mental health of the mother or that the child would be born with grave physical or mental defect, or that the pregnancy resulted from rape, incest, or other felonious intercourse. All illicit intercourse with a girl below the age of 16 shall be deemed felonious for purposes of this subsection. Justifiable abortions shall be performed only in a licensed hospital except in case of emergency when hospital facilities are unavailable. [Additional exceptions from the requirement of hospitalization may be incorporated here to take account of situations in sparsely settled areas where hospitals are not generally accessible.]

(3) *Physicians' Certificates; Presumption from Non-Compliance.* No abortion shall be performed unless two physicians, one of whom may be the person performing the abortion, shall have certified in writing the circumstances which they believe to justify the abortion. Such certificate shall be submitted before the abortion to the hospital where it is to be performed and, in the case of abortion following felonious intercourse, to the prosecuting attorney or the police. Failure to comply with any of the requirements of this Subsection gives rise to a presumption that the abortion was unjustified.

(4) *Self-Abortion.* A woman whose pregnancy has continued beyond the twenty-sixth week commits a felony of the third degree if she purposely terminates her own pregnancy otherwise than by a live birth, or if she uses instruments, drugs, or violence upon herself for

that purpose. Except as justified under Subsection (2), a person who induces or knowingly aids a woman to use instruments, drugs or violence upon herself for the purpose of terminating her pregnancy otherwise than by a live birth commits a felony of the third degree whether or not the pregnancy has continued beyond the twenty-sixth week.

(5) *Pretended Abortion.* A person commits a felony of the third degree if, representing that it is his purpose to perform an abortion, he does an act adapted to cause abortion in a pregnant woman although the woman is in fact not pregnant, or the actor does not believe she is. A person charged with unjustified abortion under Subsection (1) or an attempt to commit that offense may be convicted thereof upon proof of conduct prohibited by this Subsection.

(6) *Distribution of Abortifacients.* A person who sells, offers to sell, possesses with intent to sell, advertises, or displays for sale anything specially designed to terminate a pregnancy, or held out by the actor as useful for that purpose, commits a misdemeanor, unless:

(a) the sale, offer or display is to a physician or druggist or to an intermediary in a chain of distribution to physicians or druggists; or

(b) the sale is made upon prescription or order of a physician; or

(c) the possession is with intent to sell as authorized in paragraphs (a) and (b); or

(d) the advertising is addressed to persons named in paragraph (a) and confined to trade or professional channels not likely to reach the general public.

(7) *Section Inapplicable to Prevention of Pregnancy.* Nothing in this Section shall be deemed applicable to the prescription, administration or distribution of drugs or other substances for avoiding pregnancy, whether by preventing implantation of a fertilized ovum or by any other method that operates before, at or immediately after fertilization.

APPENDIX

From page 13:

[Summary by the Reporter:] A pregnant single woman (Roe) brought a class action challenging the constitutionality of the Texas criminal abortion laws, which proscribe procuring or attempting an abortion except on medical advice for the purpose of saving the mother's life. A licensed physician (Hallford), who had two state abortion prosecutions pending against him, was permitted to intervene. A childless married couple (the Does), the wife not being pregnant, separately attacked the laws, basing alleged injury on the future possibilities of contraceptive failure, pregnancy, unpreparedness for parenthood, and impairment of the wife's health. A three-judge District Court, which consolidated the actions, held that Roe and Hallford, and members of their classes, had standing to sue and presented justiciable controversies. Ruling that declaratory, though not injunctive, relief was warranted, the court declared the abortion statutes void as vague and overbroadly infringing those plaintiffs' Ninth and Fourteenth Amendment rights. The court ruled the Does' complaint not justiciable. Appellants directly appealed to this Court on the injunctive rulings, and appellee cross-appealed from the District Court's grant of declaratory relief to Roe and Hallford. *Held:*

1. While 28 U. S. C. § 1253 authorizes no direct appeal to this Court from the grant or denial of declaratory relief alone, review is not foreclosed when the case is properly before the Court on appeal from specific denial of injunctive relief and the arguments as to both injunctive and declaratory relief are necessarily identical. P. 123.

2. Roe has standing to sue; the Does and Hallford do not. Pp. 123–129.

(a) Contrary to appellee's contention, the natural termination of Roe's pregnancy did not moot her suit. Litigation involving pregnancy, which is "capable of repetition, yet evading review," is an exception to the usual federal rule that an actual controversy must exist at review stages and not simply when the action is initiated. Pp. 124–125.

(b) The District Court correctly refused injunctive, but erred in granting declaratory, relief to Hallford, who alleged no federally protected right not assertable as a defense against the good-faith state prosecutions pending against him. *Samuels v. Mackell,* 401 U. S. 66. Pp. 125–127.

(c) The Does' complaint, based as it is on contingencies, any one or more of which may not occur, is too speculative to present an actual case or controversy. Pp. 127–129.

3. State criminal abortion laws, like those involved here, that except from criminality only a life-saving procedure on the mother's behalf without regard to the stage of her pregnancy and other interests involved violate the Due Process Clause of the Fourteenth Amendment, which protects against state action the right to privacy, including a woman's qualified right to terminate her pregnancy. Though the State cannot override that right, it has legitimate interests in protecting both the pregnant woman's health and the potentiality of human life, each of which interests grows and reaches a "compelling" point at various stages of the woman's approach to term. Pp. 147–164.

(a) For the stage prior to approximately the end of the first trimester, the abortion decision and its effectuation must be left to the medical judgment of the pregnant woman's attending physician. Pp. 163, 164.

(b) For the stage subsequent to approximately the end of the first trimester, the State, in promoting its interest in the health of the mother, may, if it chooses, regulate the abortion procedure in ways that are reasonably related to maternal health. Pp. 163, 164.

(c) For the stage subsequent to viability the State, in promoting its interest in the potentiality of human life, may, if it chooses, regulate, and even proscribe, abortion except where necessary, in appropriate medical judgment, for the preservation of the life or health of the mother. Pp. 163–164; 164–165.

4. The State may define the term "physician" to mean only a physician currently licensed by the State, and may proscribe any abortion by a person who is not a physician as so defined. P. 165.

5. It is unnecessary to decide the injunctive relief issue since the Texas authorities will doubtless fully recognize the Court's ruling that the Texas criminal abortion statutes are unconstitutional. P. 166. 314 F. Supp. 1217, affirmed in part and reversed in part.

BLACKMUN, J., delivered the opinion of the Court, in which BURGER, C. J., and DOUGLAS, BRENNAN, STEWART, MARSHALL, and Powell, JJ., joined. BURGER, C. J., *post,* p. 207, DOUGLAS, J., *post,* p. 209, and STEWART, J., *post,* p. 167, filed concurring opinions. WHITE, J., filed a dissenting opinion, in which REHNQUIST, J., joined, *post,* p. 221. REHNQUIST, J., filed a dissenting opinion, *post,* p. 171.

Sarah Weddington reargued the cause for appellants. With her on the briefs were *Roy Lucas, Fred Bruner, Roy L. Merrill, Jr.,* and *Norman Dorsen.*

Robert C. Flowers, Assistant Attorney General of Texas, argued the cause for appellee on the reargument. *Jay Floyd,* Assistant Attorney General, argued the cause for appellee on the original argument. With them on the brief were *Crawford C. Martin,* Attorney General, *Nola White,* First Assistant Attorney General, *Alfred Walker,* Executive Assistant Attorney General, *Henry Wade,* and *John B. Tolle.**

---

*Briefs of *amici curiae* were filed by *Gary K. Nelson,* Attorney General of Arizona, *Robert K. Killian,* Attorney General of Connecticut, *Ed W. Hancock,* Attorney General of Kentucky, *Clarence A. H. Meyer,* Attorney General of Nebraska, and *Vernon B. Romney,* Attorney General of Utah; by *Joseph P. Witherspoon, Jr.,* for the Association of Texas Diocesan Attorneys; by *Charles E. Rice* for Americans United for Life; by *Eugene J. McMahon* for Women for the Unborn et al.; by *Carol Ryan* for the American College of Obstetricians and Gynecologists et al.; by *Dennis J. Horan, Jerome A. Frazel, Jr., Thomas M. Crisham,* and *Dolores V. Horan* for Certain Physicians, Professors and Fellows of the American College of Obstetrics and Gynecology; by *Harriet F. Pilpel, Nancy F. Wechsler,* and *Frederic S. Nathan* for Planned Parenthood Federation of America, Inc., et al.; by *Alan F. Charles* for the National Legal Program on Health Problems of the Poor et al.; by *Marttie L. Thompson* for State Communities Aid Assn.; by *Alfred L. Scanlan, Martin J. Flynn,* and *Robert M. Byrn* for the National Right to Life Committee; by *Helen L. Buttenwieser* for the American Ethical Union et al.; by *Norma G. Zarky* for the American Association of University Women et al.; by *Nancy Stearns* for New Women Lawyers et al.; by the California Committee to Legalize Abortion et al.; and by *Robert E. Dunne* for Robert L. Sassone.

From page 15:

[2] Ariz. Rev. Stat. Ann. § 13–211 (1956); Conn. Pub. Act No. 1 (May 1972 special session) (in 4 Conn. Leg. Serv. 677 (1972)), and Conn. Gen. Stat. Rev. §§ 53–29, 53–30 (1968) (or unborn child); Idaho Code § 18–601 (1948); Ill. Rev. Stat., c. 38, § 23–1 (1971); Ind. Code § 35–1–58–1 (1971); Iowa Code § 701.1 (1971); Ky. Rev. Stat. § 436.020 (1962); La. Rev. Stat. § 37:1285 (6) (1964) (loss of medical license) (but see § 14:87 (Supp. 1972) containing no exception for the life of the mother under the criminal statute); Me. Rev. Stat. Ann., Tit. 17, § 51 (1964); Mass. Gen. Laws Ann., c. 272, § 19 (1970) (using the term "unlawfully," construed to exclude an abortion to save the mother's life, *Kudish v. Bd. of Registration,* 356 Mass. 98, 248 N. E. 2d 264 (1969)); Mich. Comp. Laws § 750.14 (1948); Minn. Stat. § 617.18 (1971); Mo. Rev. Stat. § 559.100 (1969); Mont. Rev. Codes Ann. § 94–401 (1969); Neb. Rev. Stat. § 28–405 (1964); Nev. Rev. Stat. § 200.220 (1967); N. H. Rev. Stat. Ann. § 585:13 (1955); N. J. Stat. Ann. § 2A:87–1 (1969) ("without lawful justification"); N. D. Cent. Code §§ 12–25–01, 12–25–02 (1960); Ohio Rev. Code Ann. § 2901.16 (1953); Okla. Stat. Ann., Tit. 21, § 861 (1972–1973 Supp.); Pa. Stat. Ann., Tit. 18, §§ 4718, 4719 (1963) ("unlawful"); R. I. Gen. Laws Ann. § 11–3–1 (1969); S. D. Comp. Laws Ann. § 22–17–1 (1967); Tenn. Code Ann. §§ 39–301, 39–302 (1956); Utah Code Ann. §§ 76–2–1, 76–2–2 (1953); Vt. Stat. Ann., Tit. 13, § 101 (1958); W. Va. Code Ann. § 61–2–8 (1966); Wis. Stat. § 940.04 (1969); Wyo. Stat. Ann. §§ 6–77, 6–78 (1957).

From page 15:
Texas Laws 1854. c. 49. § 1. set forth in 3 H. Gammel. Laws of Texas 1502 (1898).

From page 15:
See Texas Penal Code of 1857, c. 7. Arts. 531–536; G. Paschal, Laws of Texas, Arts. 2192–2197 (1866); Texas *Rev.* Stat., c. 8, Arts. 536–541 (1879); Texas *Rev.* Crim. Stat., Arts. 1071–1076 (1911). The final article in each of these compilations . . .

From page 15:
[3] Long ago, a suggestion was made that the Texas statutes were unconstitutionally vague because of definitional deficiencies. The Texas Court of Criminal Appeals disposed of that suggestion peremptorily, saying only,
"It is also insisted in the motion in arrest of judgment that the statute is unconstitutional and void in that it does not sufficiently define or describe the offense of abortion. We do not concur in respect to this question." *Jackson v. State,* 55 Tex. Cr. R. 79, 89, 115 S. W. 262, 268 (1908).
The same court recently has held again that the State's abortion statutes are not unconstitutionally vague or overbroad. *Thompson v. State* (Ct. Crim. App. Tex. 1971), appeal docketed, No. 71–1200. The court held that "the State of Texas has a compelling interest to protect fetal life": that Art. 1191 "is designed to protect fetal life"; that the Texas homicide statutes, particularly Art. 1205 of the Penal Code, are intended to protect a person "in existence by actual birth" and thereby implicitly recognize other human life that is not "in existence by actual birth"; that the definition of human life is for the legislature and not the courts; that Art. 1196 "is more definite than the District of Columbia statute upheld in [*United States v.*] *Vuitch*" (402 U. S. 62); and that the Texas statute "is not vague and indefinite or overbroad." A physician's abortion conviction was affirmed.
In *Thompson,* n. 2, the court observed that any issue as to the burden of proof under the exemption of Art. 1196 "is not before us." But see *Veevers v. State,* 172 Tex. Cr. R. 162, 168–169, 354 S. W. 2nd 161, 166–167 (1962). Cf. *United States v. Vuitch,* 402 U. S. 62, 69–71 (1971).

From page 17:
Upon the filing of affidavits, motions were made for dismissal and for summary judgment. The court held that Roe and members of her class, and Dr. Hallford, had standing to sue and presented justiciable controversies, but that the Does had failed to allege facts sufficient to state a present controversy and did not have standing. It concluded that, with respect to the requests for a declaratory judgment, abstention was not warranted.

From page 17:
The court then held that abstention was warranted with respect to the requests for an injunction. It therefore dismissed the Does' complaint, declared the abortion statutes void, and dismissed the application for injunctive relief. 314 F. Supp. 1217, 1225 (ND Tex. 1970).
The plaintiffs Roe and Doe and the intervenor Hallford, pursuant to 28 U. S. C. § 1253, have appealed to this Court from that part of the District Court's judgment denying the injunction. The defendant District Attorney has purported to cross-appeal, pursuant to the same statute, from the court's grant of declaratory relief to Roe and Hallford. Both sides also have taken protective appeals to the United States Court of Appeals for the Fifth Circuit. That court ordered the appeals held in abeyance pending decision here. We postponed decision on jurisdiction to the hearing on the merits. 402 U. S. 941 (1971).

From page 17:

III

It might have been preferable if the defendant, pursuant to our Rule 20, had presented to us a petition for certiorari before judgment in the Court of Appeals with respect to the granting of the plaintiffs' prayer for declaratory relief. Our decisions in *Mitchell v. Donovan,* 398 U. S. 427 (1970), and *Gunn v. Univer-*

sity Committee, 399 U. S. 383 (1970), are to the effect that § 1253 does not authorize an appeal to this Court from the grant or denial of declaratory relief alone. We conclude, nevertheless, that those decisions do not foreclose our review of both the injunctive and the declaratory aspects of a case of this kind when it is properly here, as this one is, on appeal under § 1253 from specific denial of injunctive relief, and the arguments as to both aspects are necessarily identical. See *Carter v. Jury Comm'n,* 396 U. S. 320 (1970); *Florida Lime Growers v. Jacobsen,* 362 U. S. 73, 80–81 (1960). It would be destructive of time and energy for all concerned were we to rule otherwise. Cf. *Doe v. Bolton, post,* p. 179.

From page 17:

IV

We are next confronted with issues of justiciability, standing, and abstention. Have Roe and the Does established that "personal stake in the outcome of the controversy," *Baker v. Carr,* 369 U. S. 186, 204 (1962), that insures that "the dispute sought to be adjudicated will be presented in an adversary context and in a form historically viewed as capable of judicial resolution," *Flast v. Cohen,* 392 U. S. 83, 101 (1968), and *Sierra Club v. Morton,* 405 U. S. 727, 732 (1972)? And what effect did the pendency of criminal abortion charges against Dr. Hallford in state court have upon the propriety of the federal court's granting relief to him as a plaintiff-intervenor?

From page 18:

Abele v. Markle, 452 F. 2d, 1125 (CA2 1971), *Crossen v. Breckenridge,* 446 F 2d 833, 838–839 (CA6 1971); *Poe v. Menghini,* 339 F. Supp. 986, 990–991 (Kan. 1972). See *Truax v. Raich,* 239 U. S. 33 (1915). Indeed, we do not read the appellee's brief as really asserting anything to the contrary. The "logical nexus between the status asserted and the claim sought to be adjudicated," *Flast v. Cohen,* 302 U. S., at 102, and the necessary degree of contentiousness, *Golden v. Zwickler,* 394 U. S. 103 (1969), are both present.

From page 18:

[6] The appellee twice states in his brief that the hearing before the District Court was held on July 22, 1970. Brief for Appellee 13. The docket entries, App. 2, and the transcript, App. 76, reveal this to be an error. The July date appears to be the time of the reporter's transcription. See App. 77.

From page 19:

The usual rule in federal cases is that an actual controversy must exist at stages of appellate or certiorari review, and not simply at the date the action is initiated. *United States v. Munsingwear, Inc.,* 340 U. S. 36 (1950); *Golden v. Zwickler, supra; SEC v. Medical Committee for Human Rights,* 404 U. S. 403 (1972).

From page 19:

Pregnancy provides a classic justification for a conclusion of nonmootness. It truly could be "capable of repetition, yet evading review." *Southern Pacific Terminal Co. v. ICC,* 219 U. S. 498, 515 (1911). See *Moore v. Ogilvie,* 394 U. S. 814, 816 (1969); *Carroll v. Princess Anne,* 393 U. S. 175, 178–179 (1968); *United States v. W. T. Grant Co.,* 345 U. S. 629, 632–633 (1953).

From page 19:

... to-wit: (1) The State of Texas vs. James H. Hallford, No. C–69–5307–IH, and (2) The State of Texas vs. James H. Hallford, No. C–69–2524–H. In both cases the defendant is charged with abortion...."

In his application for leave to intervene, the doctor made like representations as to the abortion charges pending in the state court. These representations were also repeated in the affidavit he executed and filed in support of his motion for summary judgment.

Dr. Hallford is, therefore, in the position of seeking, in a federal court, declaratory and injunctive relief with respect to the same statutes under which he stands charged in criminal prosecutions simultaneously pending in state court.

From page 19:

In order to escape the rule articulated in the cases cited in the next paragraph of this opinion that, absent harassment and bad faith, a defendant in a pending state criminal case cannot affirmatively challenge in federal court the statutes under which the State is prosecuting him, Dr. Hallford seeks to distinguish his status as a present state defendant form his status as a "potential future defendant" and to assert only the latter for standing purposes here.

We see no merit in that distinction. Our decision in *Samuels v. Mackell*, 401 U. S. 66 (1971), compels the conclusion that the District Court erred when it granted declaratory relief to Dr. Hallford instead of refraining from so doing. The court, of course, was correct in refusing to grant injunctive relief to the doctor. The reasons supportive of that action, however, are those expressed in *Samuels v. Mackell, supra,* and in *Younger v. Harris,* 401 U. S. 37 (1971); *Boyle v. Landry,* 401 U. S. 77 (1971); *Perez v. Ledesma,* 401 U. S. 82 (1971); and *Byrne v. Karalexis,* 401 U. S. 216 (1971). See also *Dombrowski v. Pfister,* 380 U. S. 479 (1965). We note, in passing, that *Younger* and its companion cases were decided after the three-judge District Court decision in this case.

Dr. Hallford's complaint in intervention, therefore, is to be dismissed.[7] He is remitted to his defenses in the state criminal proceedings against him. We reverse the judgment of the District Court insofar as it granted Dr. Hallford relief and failed to dismiss his complaint in intervention.

C. *The Does.* In view of our ruling as to Roe's standing in her case, the issue of the Does' standing in their case has little significance. The claims they assert are essentially the same as those of Roe, and they attack the same statutes. Nevertheless, we briefly note the Does' posture.

---

[7] We need not consider what different result, if any, would follow if Dr. Hallford's intervention were on behalf of a class. His complaint in intervention does not purport to assert a class suit and makes no reference to any class apart from an allegation that he "and others similarly situated" must necessarily guess at the meaning of Art. 1196. His application for leave to intervene goes somewhat further, for it asserts that plaintiff Roe does not adequately protect the interest of the doctor "and the class of people who are physicians... [and] the class of people who are... patients...." The leave application, however, is not the complaint. Despite the District Court's statement to the contrary, 314 F. Supp., at 1225, we fail to perceive the essentials of a class suit in the Hallford complaint.

From page 19:

Younger v. Harris, 401 U. S., at 41–42; *Golden v. Zwickler,* 394 U. S., at 109–110; *Abele v. Markle,* 452 F. 2d, at 1124–1125; *Crossen v. Breckenridge,* 446 F. 2d, at 839. The Does' claim falls far short of those resolved otherwise in the cases that the Does urge upon us, namely, *Investment Co. Institute v. Camp,* 401 U. S. 617 (1971); *Data Processing Service v. Camp,* 397 U. S. 150 (1970); and *Epperson v. Arkansas,* 393 U. S. 97 (1968). See also *Traux v. Raich,* 239 U. S. 33 (1915).

From page 20:

[8] A. Castiglioni, A History of Medicine 84 (2d ed. 1947), E. Krumbhaar, translator and editor (hereinafter Castiglioni).

[9] J. Ricci, The Genealogy of Gynaecology 52, 84, 113, 149 (2d ed. 1950) (hereinafter Ricci); L. Lader, Abortion 75–77 (1966) (hereinafter Lader); K. Niswander, Medical Abortion Practices in the United States, in Abortion and the Law 37, 38–40 (D. Smith ed. 1967); G. Williams, The Sanctity of Life and the Criminal Law 148 (1957) (hereinafter Williams); J. Noonan, An Almost Absolute Value in History, in The Morality of Abortion 1, 3–7 (J. Noonan ed. 1970) (hereinafter Noonan); Quay, Justifiable Abortion—Medical and Legal Foundations (pt. 2), 49 Geo. L. J. 395, 406–422 (1961) (hereinafter Quay).

[10] L. Edelstein, The Hippocratic Oath 10 (1943) (hereinafter Edelstein). But see Castiglioni 227.

From page 21:

[11] Edelstein 12; Ricci 113–114, 118–119; Noonan 5.

[12] Edelstein 13–14.

[13] Castiglioni 148.

[14] *Id.*, at 154.

[15] Edelstein 3.

[16] *Id.*, at 12, 15–18.

From page 22:

[17] *Id.*, at 18; Lader 76.

[18] Edelstein 63.

[19] *Id.*, at 64.

[20] Dorland's Illustrated Medical Dictionary 1261 (24th ed. 1965).

[21] E. Coke, Institutes III *50; 1 W. Hawkins. Pleas of the Crown, c. 31, § 16 (4th ed. 1762); 1 W. Blackstone, Commentaries *129–130; M. Hale, Pleas of the Crown 433 (1st Amer. ed. 1847). For discussions of the role of the quickening concept in English common law, see Lader 78; Noonan 223–226; Means, The Law of New York Concerning Abortion and the Status of the Foetus, 1664–1968: A Case of Cessation of Constitutionality (pt 1), 14 N. Y. L. F. 411, 418–428 (1968) (hereinafter Means I); Stern, Abortion: Reform and the Law, 59 J Crim. L. C. & P. S. 84 (1968) (hereinafter Stern); Quay 430–432; Williams 152.

[22] Early philosophers believed that the embryo or fetus did not become formed and begin to live until at least 40 days after conception for a male, and 80 to 90 days for a female. See, for example, Aristotle, Hist. Anim. 7.3.583b; Gen. Anim. 2.3.736, 2.5.741; Hippocrates, Lib. de Nat. Puer., No. 10. Aristotle's thinking derived from his three-stage theory of life: vegetable, animal, rational. The vegetable stage was reached at conception, the animal at "animation," and the rational soon after live birth. This theory, together with the 40/80 day view, came to be accepted by early Christian thinkers.

The theological debate was reflected in the writings of St. Augustine, who made a distinction between *embryo inanimatus*, not yet endowed with a soul, and *embryo animatus*. He may have drawn upon Exodus 21:22. At one point, however, he expressed the view that human powers cannot determine the point during fetal development at which the critical change occurs. See Augustine, De Origine Animae 4.4 (Pub. Law 44.527). See also W. Reany, The Creation of the Human Soul, c. 2 and 83–86 (1932); Huser, The Crime of Abortion in Canon Law 15 (Catholic Uni*v*. of America, Canon Law Studies No. 162, Washington, D. C., 1942).

Galen, in three treatises related to embryology, accepted the thinking of Aristotle and his followers. Quay 426–427. Later, Augustine on abortion was incorporated by Gratian into the Decretum, published about 1140. Decretum Magistri Gratiani 2.32.2.7 to 2.32.2.10, in 1 Corpus Juris Canonici 1122, 1123 (A. Friedburg, 2d ed. 1879). This Decretal and the Decretals that followed were recognized as the definitive body of canon law until the new Code of 1917.

For discussions of the canon-law treatment, see Means I, pp. 411–412; Noonan 20–26; Quay 426–430; see also J. Noonan, Contraception: A History of Its Treatment by the Catholic Theologians and Canonists 18–29 (1965).

From page 23:

[23] Bracton took the position that abortion by blow or poison was homicide "if the foetus be already formed and animated, and particularly if it be animated." 2 H. Bracton, De Legibus et Consuetudinibus Angliae 279 (T. Twiss ed. 1879), or, as a later translation puts it, "if the foetus is already formed or quickened, especially if it is quickened," 2 H. Bracton, On the Laws and Customs of England 341 (S. Thorne ed. 1968). See Quay 431; see also 2 Fleta 60–61 (Book 1, c. 23) (Selden Society ed. 1955).

[24] E. Coke, Institutes III *50.

[25] 1 W. Blackstone, Commentaries *129–130.

[27] *Commonwealth v. Bangs*, 9 Mass. 387, 388 (1812); *Commonwealth v. Parker*, 50 Mass. (9 Metc.) 263, 265–266 (1845); *State v. Cooper*, 22 N. J. L. 52, 58 (1849); *Abrams v. Foshee*, 3 Iowa 274, 278–280 (1856); *Smith v. Gaffard*, 31 Ala. 45, 51 (1857); *Mitchell v. Commonwealth*, 78 Ky. 204, 210 (1879);

Eggart v. State, 40 Fla. 527, 532, 25 So. 144, 145 (1898); *State v. Alcorn*, 7 Idaho 599, 606, 64 P. 1014, 1016 (1901); *Edwards v. State*, 79 Neb. 251, 252, 112 N. W. 611, 612 (1907); *Gray v. State*, 77 Tex. Cr. R. 221, 224, 178 S. W. 337, 338 (1915); *Miller v. Bennett*, 190 Va. 162, 169, 56 S. E. 2d 217, 221 (1949). Contra, *Mills v. Commonwealth*, 13 Pa. 631, 633 (1850); *State v. Slagle*, 83 N. C. 630, 632 (1880).

[28] See *Smith v. State*, 33 Me. 48, 55 (1851); *Evans v. People*, 49 N. Y. 86, 88 (1872); *Lamb v. State*, 67 Md. 524, 533, 10 A. 208 (1887).

From page 24:

43 Geo. 3, c. 58 . . . . 9 Geo. r.c. 31 § 13 . . . 7 Will. 4 & 1 Vict., c. 85, § 6, . . . 24 & 25 Vict., c. 100, § 59, . . . 19 & 20 Geo. 5, c. 34 . . . 1 K. B. 687.

From page 25:

15 & 16 Eliz. 2, c. 87

[29] Conn. Stat., Tit. 20, § 14 (1821).

[30] Conn. Pub. Acts, c. 71, § 1 (1860).

[31] N. Y. Rev. Stat., pt. 4, c. 1, Tit. 2, Art. 1, § 9, p. 661, and Tit. 6, § 21, p. 694 (1829).

[32] Act of Jan. 20, 1840, § 1, set forth in 2 H. Gammel, Laws of Texas 177–178 (1898); see *Grigsby v. Reib*, 105 Tex. 597, 600, 153 S. W. 1124, 1125 (1913).

[33] The early statutes are discussed on Quay 435–438. See also Lader 85–88; Stern 85–86; and Means II 375–376.

From page 26:

[35] Ala. Code, Tit. 14, § 9 (1958); D. C. Code Ann. § 22–201 (1967).

[36] Mass. Gen. Laws Ann., c. 272, § 19 (1970); N. J. Stat. Ann. § 2A:87–1 (1969); Pa. Stat. Ann., Tit. 18, §§ 4718, 4719 (1963).

From page 26:

[37] Fourteen States have adopted some form of the ALI statute. See Ark. Stat. Ann. §§ 41–303 to 41–310 (Supp. 1971); Calif. Health & Safety Code §§ 25950–25955.5 (Supp. 1972); Colo. Rev. Stat. Ann. §§ 40–2–50 to 40–2–53 (Cum. Supp. 1967); Del. Code Ann., Tit. 24, §§ 1790–1793 (Supp. 1972); Florida Law of Apr. 13, 1972, c. 72–196, 1972 Fla. Sess. Law Serv., pp. 380–382; Ga. Code §§ 26–1201 to 26–1203 (1972); Kan. Stat. Ann. § 21–3407 (Supp. 1971); Md. Ann. Code, Art. 43, §§ 137–139 (1971); Miss. Code Ann. § 2223 (Supp. 1972); N. M. Stat. Ann. §§ 40A–5–1 to 40A–5–3 (1972); N. C. Gen. Stat. § 14–45.1 (Supp. 1971); Ore. Rev. Stat. §§ 435.405 to 435.495 (1971); S. C. Code Ann. §§ 16–82 to 16–89 (1962 and Supp. 1971); Va. Code Ann. §§ 18.1–62 to 18.1–62.3 (Supp. 1972). Mr. Justice Clark described some of these States as having "led the way." Religion, Morality, and Abortion: A Constitutional Appraisal, 2 Loyola U. (L. A.) L. Rev. 1, 11 (1969).

By the end of 1970, four other States had repealed criminal penalties for abortions performed in early pregnancy by a licensed physician, subject to stated procedural and health requirements. Alaska Stat. § 11.15.060 (1970); Haw. Rev. Stat. § 453–16 (Supp. 1971); N. Y. Penal Code § 125.05, subd. 3 (Supp. 1972–1973); Wash. Rev. Code §§ 9.02.060 to 9.02.080 (Supp. 1972). The precise status of criminal abortion laws in some States is made unclear by recent decisions in state and federal courts striking down existing state laws, in whole or in part.

From page 29:

[38] "Whereas, Abortion, like any other medical procedure, should not be performed when contrary to the best interests of the patient since good medical practice requires due consideration for the patient's welfare and not mere acquiescence to the patient's demand; and

"Whereas, The standards of sound clinical judgment, which, together with informed patient consent should be determinative according to the merits of each individual case; therefore be it

"*RESOLVED*, That abortion is a medical procedure and should be performed only by a duly licensed physician and surgeon in an accredited hospital acting only after consultation with two other physicians chosen because of their professional competency and in conformance with standards of good medical practice and the Medical Practice Act of his State; and be it further

"*RESOLVED*, That no physician or other professional personnel shall be compelled to perform any act which violates his good medical judgment. Neither physician, hospital, nor hospital personnel shall be required to perform any act violative of personally-held moral principles. In these circumstances good medical practice requires only that the physician or other professional personnel withdraw from the case so long as the withdrawal is consistent with good medical practice." Proceedings of the AMA House of Delegates 220 (June 1970).

[39] "The Principles of Medical Ethics of the AMA do not prohibit a physician from performing an abortion that is performed in accordance with good medical practice and under circumstances that do not violate the laws of the community in which he practices.

"In the matter of abortions, as of any other medical procedure, the Judicial Council becomes involved whenever there is alleged violation of the Principles of Medical Ethics as established by the House of Delegates."

From page 30:

[40] "UNIFORM ABORTION ACT

"SECTION 1. [*Abortion Defined; When Authorized.*]

"(a) 'Abortion' means the termination of human pregnancy with an intention other than to produce a live birth or to remove a dead fetus.

"(b) An abortion may be performed in this state only if it is performed:

"(1) by a physician licensed to practice medicine [or osteopathy] in this state or by a physician practicing medicine [or osteopathy] in the employ of the government of the United States or of this state, [and the abortion is performed [in the physician's office or in a medical clinic, or] in a hospital approved by the [Department of Health] or operated by the United States, this state, or any department, agency, or political subdivision of either;] or by a female upon herself upon the advice of the physician; and

"(2) within [20] weeks after the commencement of the pregnancy [or after [20] weeks only if the physician has reasonable cause to believe (i) there is a substantial risk that continuance of the pregnancy would endanger the life of the mother or would gravely impair the physical or mental health of the mother, (ii) that the child would be born with grave physical or mental defect, or (iii) that the pregnancy resulted from rape or incest, or illicit intercourse with a girl under the age of 16 years].

"SECTION 2. [*Penalty.*] Any person who performs or procures an abortion other than authorized by this Act is guilty of a [felony] and, upon conviction thereof, may be sentenced to pay a fine not exceeding [$1,000] or to imprisonment [in the state penitentiary] not exceeding [5 years], or both.

"SECTION 3. [*Uniformity of Interpretation.*] This Act shall be construed to effectuate its general purpose to make uniform the law with respect to the subject of this Act among those states which enact it.

"SECTION 4. [*Short Title.*] This Act may be cited as the Uniform Abortion Act.

"SECTION 5. [*Severability.*] If any provision of this Act or the application thereof to any person or circumstance is held invalid, the invalidity does not affect other provisions or applications of this Act which can be given effect without the invalid provision or application, and to this end the provisions of this Act are severable.

"SECTION 6. [*Repeal.*] The following acts and parts of acts are repealed:

"(1)

"(2)

"(3)

"Section 7. [Time of Taking Effect.] This Act shall take effect _____."

From page 31:

[42] See, for example, *YWCA v. Kugler,* 342 F. Supp. 1048, 1074 (N. J. 1972); *Abele v. Markle,* 342 F. Supp. 800, 805–806 (Conn. 1972) (Newman, J., concurring in result), appeal docketed, No. 72–56; *Walsingham v. State,* 250 So. 2d 857, 863 (Ervin, J., concurring) (Fla. 1971); *State v. Gedicke,* 43 N. J. L. 86, 90 (1881); Means II 381–382.

[43] See C. Haagensen & W. Lloyd, A Hundred Years of Medicine 19 (1943).

[44] Potts, Postconceptive Control of Fertility, 8 Int'l J. of G. & O. 957, 967 (1970) (England and Wales); Abortion Mortality, 20 Morbidity and Mortality 208, 209 (June 12, 1971) (U. S. Dept. of HEW, Public Health Service) (New York City); Tietze, United States: Therapeutic Abortions, 1963–1968, 59 Studies in Family Planning 5, 7 (1970); Tietze, Mortality with Contraception and Induced Abortion, 45 Studies in Family Planning 6 (1969) (Japan, Czechoslovakia, Hungary); Tietze & Lehfeldt, Legal Abortion in Eastern Europe, 175 J. A. M. A. 1149, 1152 (April 1961). Other sources are discussed in Lader 17–23.

From page 32:

[45] See Brief of *Amicus* National Right to Live Committee; R. Drinan, The Inviolability of the Right to Be Born, in Abortion and the Law 107 (D. Smith ed. 1967); Louisell, Abortion, The Practice of Medicine and the Due Process of Law, 16 U. C. L. A. L. Rev., 233 (1969); Noonan I.

[46] See, *e. g., Abele v. Markle,* 342 F. Supp. 800 (Conn. 1972), appeal docketed, No. 72–56.

From page 33:

[47] See discussions in Means I and Means II.

[48] See, *e. g., State v. Murphy,* 27 N. J. L. 112, 114 (1858).

[49] *Watson v. State,* 9 Tex. App. 237, 244–245 (1880); *Moore v. State,* 37 Tex. Cr. R. 552, 561, 40 S. W. 287, 290 (1897); *Shaw v. State,* 73 Tex. Cr. R. 337, 339, 165 S. W. 930, 931 (1914); *Fondren v. State,* 74 Tex. Cr. R. 552, 557, 169 S. W. 411, 414 (1914); *Gray v. State,* 77 Tex. Cr. R. 221, 229, 178 S. W. 337, 341 (1915). There is no immunity in Texas for the father who is not married to the mother. *Hammett v. State,* 84 Tex. Cr. R. 635, 209 S. W. 661 (1919); *Thompson v. State* (Ct. Crim. App. Tex. 1971), appeal docketed, No. 71–1200.

[50] See *Smith v. State,* 33 Me., at 55; *In re Vince,* 2 N. J. 443, 450, 67 A. 2d 141, 144 (1949). A short discussion of the modern law on this issue is contained in the Comment to the ALI's Model Penal Code § 207.11, at 158 and nn. 35–37 (Tent. Draft No. 9, 1959).

From page 35:

Abele v. Markle, 352 F. Supp. 800 (Conn. 1972), appeal docketed, No. 72–56; *Abele v. Markle,* 351 F. Supp. 224 (Conn. 1972), appeal docketed, No. 72–730; *Doe v. Bolton,* 319 F. Supp. 1048 (ND Ga. 1970), appeal decided today, *post,* p. 179; *Doe v. Scott,* 321 F. Supp. 1385 (ND Ill. 1971), appeal docketed, No. 70–105; *Poe v. Menghini,* 339 F. Supp. 986 (Kan. 1972); *YWCA v. Kugler,* 342 F. Supp. 1048 (NJ 1972); *Babbitz v. McCann,* 310 F. Supp. 293 (ED Wis. 1970), appeal dismissed. 400 U. S. 1 (1970); *People v. Belous,* 71 Cal. 2d 954, 458 P. 2d 194 (1969), cert. denied, 397 U. S. 915 (1970); *State v. Barquet,* 262 So. 2d 431 (Fla. 1972).

From page 35:

Crossen v. Attorney General, 344 F. Supp. 587 (ED Ky. 1972), appeal docketed, No. 72–256; *Rosen v. Louisiana State Board of Medical Examiners,* 318 F. Supp. 1217 (ED La. 1970), appeal docketed, Nol 70–42; *Corkey v. Edwards,* 322 F. Supp. 1248 (WDNC 1971), appeal docketed, No. 71–92; *Steinberg v. Brown,* 321 F. Supp. 741 (ND Ohio 1970); *Doe v. Rampton* (Utah 1971), appeal docketed, No. 71–5666; *Cheaney v. State,* ——— Ind. ———, 285 N. E. 2d 265 (1972); *Spears v. State,* 257 So. 2d 876 (Miss. 1972); *State v. Munson,* 86 S. D. 663, 201 N. W. 2d 123 (1972), appeal docketed, No. 72–631.

Frompage 36:

⁵¹ Tr. of Oral Rearg. 20–21.

⁵² Tr. of Oral Rearg. 24.

From page 38:

McGarvey v. Magee-Womens Hospital, 340 F. Supp. 751 (WD Pa. 1972); *Byrn v. New York City Health & Hospitals Corp.*, 31 N. Y. 2d 194, 286 N. E. 2d 887 (1972), appeal docketed, No. 72–434; *Abele v. Markle,* 351 F. Supp. 224 (Conn. 1972), appeal docketed, No. 72–730. Cf. *Cheaney v. State,* —— Ind., at ——, 285 N. E. 2d, at 270; *Montana v. Rogers,* 278 F. 2d 68, 72 (CA7 1960), aff'd *sub nom Montana v. Kennedy,* 366 U. S. 308 (1961); *Keeler v. Superior Court,* 2 Cal. 3d 619, 470 P. 2d 617 (1970); *State v. Dickinson,* 28 Ohio St. 2d 65, 275 N. E. 2d 599 (1971).

From page 39:

⁵⁶ Edelstein 16.

⁵⁷ Lader 97–99; D. Feldman, Birth Control in Jewish Law 251–294 (1968). For a stricter view, see I. Jakobovits, Jewish Views on Abortion, in Abortion and the Law 124 (D. Smith ed. 1967).

⁵⁸ Amicus Brief for the American Ethical Union et al. For the position of the National Council of Churches and of other denominations, see Lader 99–101.

⁵⁹ L. Hellman & J. Pritchard, Williams Obstetrics 493 (14th ed. 1971); Dorland's Illustrated Medical Dictionary 1968 (24th ed. 1965).

⁶⁰ Hellman & Pritchard, *supra,* n. 59, at 493.

⁶¹ For discussions of the development of the Roman Catholic position, see D. Callahan, Abortion: Law, Choice, and Morality 409–447 (1970); Noonan 1.

⁶² See Brodie, The New Biology and the Prenatal Child, 9 J. Family L. 391, 397 (1970); Gorney, The New Biology and the Future of Man, 15 U. C. L. A. L. Rev. 273 (1968); Note, Criminal Law—Abortion—The "Morning-After Pill" and Other Pre-Implantation Birth-Control Methods and the Law, 46 Ore. L. Rev. 211 (1967); G. Taylor, The Biological Time Bomb 32 (1968); A. Rosenfeld, The Second Genesis 138–139 (1969); Smith, Through a Test Tube Darkly: Artificial Insemination and the Law, 67 Mich. L. Rev. 127 (1968); Note, Artificial Insemination and the Law, 1968 U. Ill. L. F. 203.

⁶³ W. Prosser, The Law of Torts 335–338 (4th ed. 1971); 2 F. Harper & F. James, The Law of Torts 1028–1031 (1956); Note, 63 Harv. L. Rev. 173 (1949).

From page 40:

⁶⁴ See cases cited in Prosser, *supra,* n. 63, at 336–338; Annotation, Action for Death of Unborn Child. 15 A. L. R. 3d 992 (1967).

⁶⁵ Prosser, *supra,* n. 63, at 338; Note, The Law and the Unborn Child: The Legal and Logical Inconsistencies, 46 Notre Dame Law. 349, 354–360 (1971).

⁶⁶ Louisell, Abortion, The Practice of Medicine and the Due Process of Law, 16 U. C. L. A. L. Rev. 233, 235–238 (1969); Note, 56 Iowa L. Rev. 994, 999–1000 (1971); Note, The Law and the Unborn Child, 46 Notre Dame Law. 349, 351–354 (1971).

From page 43:

The Court has recognized that different considerations enter into a federal court's decision as to declaratory relief, on the one hand, and injunctive relief, on the other. *Zwickler v. Koota,* 389 U. S. 241, 252–255 (1967); *Dombrowski v. Pfister,* 380 U. S. 479 (1965). We are not dealing with a statute that, on its face, appears to abridge free expression, an area of particular concern under *Dombrowski* and refined in *Younger v. Harris,* 401 U. S., at 50.

From page 49:

[1] Jurisdictions having enacted abortion laws prior to the adoption of the Fourteenth Amendment in 1868:

1. Alabama—Ala. Acts, c. 6, § 2 (1840).

2. Arizona—Howell Code, c. 10, § 45 (1865).

3. Arkansas—Ark. Rev. Stat., c. 44, div. III, Art. II, § 6 (1838).

4. California—Cal. Sess. Laws, c. 99, § 45, p. 233 (1849–1850).

5. Colorado (Terr.)—Colo. Gen. Laws of Terr. of Colo., 1st Sess., § 42, pp. 296–297 (1861).

6. Connecticut—Conn. Stat., Tit. 20, §§ 14, 16 (1821). By 1868, this statute had been replaced by another abortion law. Conn. Pub. Acts, c. 71, §§ 1, 2, p. 65 (1860).

7. Florida—Fla. Acts 1st Sess., c. 1637, subc. 3, §§ 10, 11, subc. 8, §§ 9, 10, 11 (1868), as amended, now Fla. Stat. Ann. §§ 782.09, 782.10, 797.01, 797.02, 782.16 (1965).

8. Georgia—Ga. Pen. Code, 4th Div., § 20 (1833).

9. Kingdom of Hawaii—Hawaii Pen. Code, c. 12, §§ 1, 2, 3 (1850).

10. Idaho (Terr.)—Idaho (Terr.) Laws, Crimes and Punishments §§ 33, 34, 42, pp. 441, 443 (1863).

11. Illinois—Ill. Rev. Criminal Code §§ 40, 41, 46, pp. 130, 131 (1827). By 1868, this statute had been replaced by a subsequent enactment. Ind. Laws §§ 1, 2, 3, p. 89 (1867).

12. Indiana—Ind. Rev. Stat. §§ 1, 3, p. 224 (1838). By 1868 this statute had been superseded by a subsequent enactment. Ill. Pub. Laws, c. LXXXI, § 2 (1859).

13. Iowa (Terr.)—Iowa (Terr.) Stat., 1st Legis., 1st Sess., § 18, p. 145 (1838). By 1868, this statute had been superseded by a subsequent enactment. Iowa (Terr.) Rev. Stat., c. 49, §§ 10, 13 (1843).

14. Kansas (Terr.)—Kan. (Terr.) Stat., c. 48, §§ 9, 10, 39 (1855). By 1868, this statute had been superseded by a subsequent enactment. Kan. (Terr.) Laws, c. 28, §§ 9, 10, 37 (1859).

15. Louisiana—La. Rev. Stat., Crimes and Offenses § 24, p. 138 (1856).

16. Maine—Me. Rev. Stat., c. 160, §§ 11, 12, 13, 14 (1840).

17. Maryland—Md. Laws, c. 179, § 2, p. 315 (1868).

18. Massachusetts—Mass. Acts & Resolves, c. 27 (1845).

19. Michigan—Mich. Rev. Stat., c. 153, §§ 32, 33, 34, p. 662 (1846).

20. Minnesota (Terr.)—Minn. (Terr.) Rev. Stat., c. 100, §§ 10, 11, p. 493 (1851).

21. Mississippi—Miss. Code, c. 64, §§ 8, 9, p. 958 (1848).

22. Missouri—Mo. Rev. Stat., Art. II, §§ 9, 10, 36, pp. 168, 172 (1835).

23. Montana (Terr.)—Mont. (Terr.) Laws, Criminal Practice Acts § 41, p. 184 (1864).

24. Nevada (Terr.)—Nev. (Terr.) Laws, c. 28, § 42, p. 63 (1861).

25. New Hampshire—N. H. Laws, c. 743, § 1, p. 708 (1848).

26. New Jersey—N. J. Laws, p. 266 (1849).

27. New York—N. Y. Rev. Stat., pt. 4, c. 1, Tit. 2, §§ 8, 9, pp. 12–13 (1828). By 1868, this statute had been superseded. N. Y. Laws, c. 260, §§ 1–6, pp. 285–286 (1845); N. Y. Laws, c. 22, § 1, p. 19 (1846).

28. Ohio—Ohio Gen. Stat. §§ 111 (1), 112 (2), p. 252 (1841).

29. Oregon—Ore. Gen. Laws, Crim. Code, c. 43, § 509, p. 528 (1845–1864).

30. Pennsylvania—Pa. Laws No. 374, §§ 87, 88, 89 (1860).

31. Texas—Tex. Gen. Stat. Dig., c. VII, Arts. 531–536, p. 524 (Oldham & White 1859).

32. Vermont—Vt. Acts No. 33, § 1 (1846). By 1868, this statute had been amended. Vt. Acts No. 57, §§ 1, 3 (1867).

33. Virginia—Va. Acts, Tit. II, c. 3, §9, p. 96 (1848).

34. Washington (Terr.)—Wash. (Terr.) Stats., c. II, §§ 37, 38, p. 81 (1854).

35. West Virginia—See Va. Acts., Tit. II, c. 3, § 9, p. 96 (1848); W. Va. Const., Art. XI, par. 8 (1863).

36. Wisconsin—Wis. Rev. Stat., c. 133, §§ 10, 11 (1849). By 1868, this statute had been superseded. Wis. Rev. Stat., c. 164, §§ 10, 11; c. 169, §§ 58, 59 (1858).

[2] Abortion laws in effect in 1868 and still applicable as of August 1970:

1. Arizona (1865).
2. Connecticut (1860).
3. Florida (1868).
4. Idaho (1863).
5. Indiana (1838).
6. Iowa (1843).
7. Maine (1840).
8. Massachusetts (1845).
9. Michigan (1846).
10. Minnesota (1851).
11. Missouri (1835).
12. Montana (1864).
13. Nevada (1861).
14. New Hampshire (1848).
15. New Jersey (1849).
16. Ohio (1841).
17. Pennsylvania (1860).
18. Texas (1859).
19. Vermont (1867).
20. West Virginia (1863).
21. Wisconsin (1858).

From page 51:

[Summary by the Reporter:] Georgia law proscribes an abortion except as performed by a duly licensed Georgia physician when necessary in "his best clinical judgment" because continued pregnancy would endanger a pregnant woman's life or injure her health; the fetus would likely be born with a serious defect; or the pregnancy resulted from rape. § 26–1202 (a) of Ga. Criminal Code. In addition to a requirement that the patient be a Georgia resident and certain other requirements, the statutory scheme poses three procedural conditions in § 26–1202 (b): (1) that the abortion be performed in a hospital accredited by the Joint Commission on Accreditation of Hospitals (JCAH); (2) that the procedure by approved by the hospital staff abortion committee; and (3) that the performing physician's judgment be confirmed by independent examinations of the patient by two other licensed physicians. Appellant Doe, an indigent married Georgia citizen, who was denied an abortion after eight weeks of pregnancy for failure to meet any of the § 26–1202 (a) conditions, sought declaratory and injunctive relief, contending that the Georgia laws were unconstitutional. Others joining in the complaint included Georgia-licensed physicians (who claimed that the Georgia statutes "chilled and deterred" their practices), registered nurses, clergymen, and social workers. Though holding that all the plaintiffs had standing, the District Court ruled that only Doe presented a justiciable controversy. In Doe's case the court gave declaratory, but not injunctive, relief, invalidating as an infringement of privacy and personal liberty the limitation to the three situations specified in §26–1202 (a) and certain other provisions but holding that the State's interest in health protection and the existence of a "*potential* of independent human existence" justified regulation through § 26–1202 (b) of the "manner of performance as well as the quality of the final decision to abort." The appellants, claiming entitlement to broader relief, directly appealed to this Court. *Held*:

1. Doe's case presents a live, justiciable controversy and she has standing to sue, *Roe v. Wade, ante,* p. 113 as do the physician-appellants (who, unlike the physician in *Wade,* were not charged with abortion violations), and it is therefore unnecessary to resolve the issue of the other appellants' standing. Pp. 187–189.

2. A woman's constitutional right to an abortion is not absolute. *Roe v. Wade, supra.* P. 189.

3. The requirement that a physician's decision to perform an abortion must rest upon "his best clinical judgment" of its necessity is not unconstitutionally vague, since that judgment may be made in the

light of *all* the attendant circumstances. *United States v. Vuitch*, 402 U. S. 62, 71–72. Pp. 191–192.

4. The three procedural conditions in § 26–1202 (b) violate the Fourteenth Amendment. Pp. 192–200.

(a) The JCAH-accreditation requirement is invalid, since the State has not shown that only hospitals (let alone those with JCAH accreditation) meet its interest in fully protecting the patient; and a hospital requirement failing to exclude the first trimester of pregnancy would be invalid on that ground alone, see *Roe v. Wade, supra.* Pp. 193–195.

(b) The interposition of a hospital committee on abortion, a procedure not applicable as a matter of state criminal law to other surgical situations, is unduly restrictive of the patient's rights, which are already safeguarded by her personal physician. Pp. 195–198.

(c) Required acquiescence by two copractitioners also has no rational connection with a patient's needs and unduly infringes on her physician's right to practice. Pp. 198–200.

5. The Georgia residence requirement violates the Privileges and Immunities Clause by denying protection to persons who enter Georgia for medical services there. P. 200.

6. Appellants' equal protection argument centering on the three procedural conditions in § 26–1202 (b), invalidated on other grounds, is without merit. Pp. 200–201.

7. No ruling is made on the question of injunctive relief. Cf. *Roe v. Wade, supra.* P. 201.
319 F. Supp. 1048, modified and affirmed.

From page 51:

BLACKMUN, J., delivered the opinion of the Court, in which BURGER, C. J., and DOUGLAS, BRENNAN, STEWART, MARSHALL, and POWELL, JJ., joined. BURGER, C. J., *post.* p. 207, and DOUGLAS, J., *post,* p. 209, filed concurring opinions. WHITE, J., filed a dissenting opinion, in which REHNQUIST, J., joined, *post,* p. 221. REHNQUIST, J., filed a dissenting opinion, *post.* p. 223.

Margie Pitts Hames reargued the case for appellants. With her on the briefs were *Reber F. Boult, Jr., Charles Morgan, Jr., Elizabeth Roediger Rindskopf,* and *Tobiane Schwartz.*

Dorothy T. Beasley reargued the cause for appellees. With her on the brief were *Arthur K. Bolton,* Attorney General of Georgia, *Harold N. Hill, Jr.,* Executive Assistant Attorney General, *Courtney Wilder Stanton,* Assistant Attorney General, *Joel Feldman, Henry L. Bowden,* and *Ralph H. Witt.**

---

*Briefs of *amici curiae* were filed by *Roy Lucas* for the American College of Obstetricians and Gynecologists et al.; by *Dennis J. Horan, Jerome A. Frazel, Jr., Thomas M. Crisham,* and *Delores V. Horan* for Certain Physicians, Professors and Fellows of the American College of Obstetrics and Gynecology; by *Harriet F. Pilpel, Nancy F. Wechsler,* and *Frederic S. Nathan* for Planned Parenthood Federation of America, Inc., et al.; by *Alan F. Charles* for the National Legal Program on Health Problems of the Poor et al.; by *Marttie L. Thompson* for State Communities Aid Assn.; by *Alfred L. Scanlan, Martin J. Flynn,* and *Robert M. Byrn* for the National Right to Life Committee; by *Helen L. Buttenwieser* for the American Ethical Union et al.; by *Norma G. Zarky* for the American Association of University Women et al.; by *Nancy Stearns* for New Women Lawyers et al.; by the California Committee to Legalize Abortion et al.; by *Robert E. Dunne* for Robert L. Sassone; and by *Ferdinand Buckley pro se.*

From page 52:

[1] The portions italicized in Appendix A are those held unconstitutional by the District Court.
[2] Brief for Appellants 25 n. 5; Tr. of Oral Arg. 9.
[3] See *Roe v. Wade, ante.* p. 113, at 140 n. 37.
[4] The pertinent provisions of the 1876 statute were:

"Section I. *Be it enacted, etc.,* That from and after the passage of this Act, the wilful killing of an unborn child, so far developed as to be ordinarily called 'quick,' by any injury to the mother of such child, which would be murder if it resulted in the death of such mother, shall be guilty of a felony, and punishable by death or imprisonment for life, as the jury trying the case may recommend.

"Sec. II. *Be it further enacted,* That every person who shall administer to any woman pregnant with a child, any medicine, drug, or substance whatever, or shall use or employ any instrument or other means, with intent thereby to destroy such child, unless the same shall have been necessary to preserve the life of such mother, or shall have been advised by two physicians to be necessary for such purpose, shall, in case the death of such child or mother be thereby produced, be declared guilty of an assault with intent to murder.

"Sec. III. *Be it further enacted,* That any person who shall wilfully administer to any pregnant woman any medicine, drug or substance, or anything whatever, or shall employ any instrument or means whatever, with intent thereby to procure the miscarriage or abortion of any such woman, unless the same shall have been necessary to preserve the life of such woman, or shall have been advised by two physicians to be necessary for that purpose, shall, upon conviction, be punished as prescribed in section 4310 of the Revised Code of Georgia."

It should be noted that the second section, in contrast to the first, made no specific reference to quickening. The section was construed, however, to possess this line of demarcation. *Taylor v. State,* 105 Ga. 846, 33 S. E. 190 (1899).

From page 54:

The case was then tried on the pleadings and interrogatories.

The District Court, *per curiam,* 319 F. Supp. 1048 (ND Ga. 1970), held that only Doe presented a justiciable controversy On the merits...

From page 55:

...pursuant to 28 U. S. C. § 1253. We postponed decision on jurisdiction to the hearing on the merits. 402 U. S. 941 (1971). The defendants also purported to appeal, pursuant to § 1253, but their appeal was dismissed for want of jurisdiction. 402 U. S. 936 (1971). We are advised by the appellees, Brief 42, that an alternative appeal on their part is pending in the United States Court of Appeals for the Fifth Circuit. The extent, therefore, to which the District Court decision was adverse to the defendants, that is, the extent to which portions of the Georgia statutes were held to be unconstitutional, technically is not now before us.[8] *Swarb v. Lennox,* 405 U. S. 191, 201 (1972).

[8] What we decide today obviously has implications for the issues raised in the defendants' appeal pending in the Fifth Circuit.

From page 56:

Crossen v. Breckenridge, 446 F. 2d 833, 839–840 (CA6 1971); *Poe v. Menghini,* 339 F. Supp. 986, 990–991 (Kan. 1972)

In holding that the physicians, while theoretically possessed of standing, did not present a justiciable controversy, the District Court seems to have relied primarily on *Poe v. Ullman,* 367 U. S. 497 (1961). There, a sharply divided Court dismissed an appeal from a state court on the ground that it presented no real controversy justifying the adjudication of a constitutional issue.

From page 56:

The present case, therefore, is closer to *Epperson v. Arkansas,* 393 U. S. 97 (1968), where the Court recognized the right of a school teacher, though not yet charged criminally, to challenge her State's anti-evolution statute. See also *Griswold v. Connecticut,* 381 U.S., at 481.

From page 60:

[14] See *Roe v. Wade, ante,* at 146–147, n. 40.

[15] Some state statutes do not have the JCAH-accreditation requirement. Alaska Stat. § 11.15.060 (1970); Hawaii Rev. Stat. § 453–16 (Supp. 1971); N. Y. Penal Code § 125.05, subd. 3 (Supp. 1972–1973). Washington has the requirement but couples it with the alternative of "a medical facility

approved...by the state board of health." Wash. Rev. Code § 9.02.070 (Supp. 1972); Florida's new statute has a similar provision. Law of Apr. 13, 1972, c. 72–196. § 1 (2). Others contain the specification. Ark. Stat. Ann. §§41–303 to 41–310 (Supp. 1971); Calif. Health & Safety Code §§ 25950–25955.5 (Supp. 1972); Colo. Rev. Stat. Ann. §§ 40–2–50 to 40–2–53 (Cum. Supp. 1967); Kan. Stat. Ann. § 21–3407 (Supp. 1971); Md. Ann. Code, Art. 43, §§ 137–139 (1971). Cf. Del. Code Ann., Titl. 24, §§ 1790–1793 (Supp. 1972), specifying "a nationally recognized medical or hospital accreditation authority" § 1790 (a).

From page 63:

[16] L. Baker & M. Freeman, Abortion Surveillance at Grady Memorial Hospital Center for Disease Control (June and July 1971) (U. S. Dept. of HEW, Public Health Service).

From pages 73–74:

Abortion Morality, 20 Morbidity and Mortality 208, 209 (June 1971) (U. S. Dept. of HEW, Public Health Service). On the other hand, the maternal mortality rate associated with childbirths other than abortions was 18 per 100,000 live births. Tietze, Mortality with Contraception and Induced Abortion, 45 Studies in Family Planning 6 (1969). See also Tietze & Lehfeldt, Legal Abortion in Eastern Europe, 175 J. A. M. A. 1149, 1152 (Apr. 1961); Kolblova, Legal Abortion in Czechoslovakia, 196 J. A. M. A. 371 (Apr. 1966); Mehland, Combating Illegal Abortion in the Socialist Countries of Europe, 13 World Med. J. 84 (1966).

[6] Religion, Morality, and Abortion: A Constitutional Appraisal, 2 Loyola U. (L. A.) L. Rev. 1, 9–10 (1969).

From page 75:

[8] See Ga. Code Ann. § 26–1202 (b) (3).
[9] See id., § 26–1202 (b) (4).
[10] Id., § 26–1202 (b) (5).

From page 76:

[11] See Rochat, Tyler, & Schoenbucher, An Epidemiological Analysis of Abortion in Georgia, 61 Am. J. of Public Health 543 (1971).
[12] Supra, n. 6, at 10.

POSTSCRIPT

Since the decisions in *Roe v. Wade* and *Doe v. Bolton*, the Supreme Court has handed down the following rulings regarding legislation that regulates abortion. This Postscript sets forth the holdings—the decisions—in those cases. The Justices have expressed their reasoning in support of their positions in many majority, concurring, and dissenting opinions.

Planned Parenthood of Central Missouri v. Danforth, 428 U. S. 52 (1976)

Challenges to a Missouri statute led to the following decisions:

The definition of "viability" as that stage of fetal development when the life of the unborn child may be continued outside the womb naturally or with artificial support systems was found constitutional under *Roe v. Wade.* The requirement that the woman sign a form that her consent is "informed and freely given and not the result of coercion" was also found to be permissible. Certain record-keeping requirements, similar to those used with respect to other medical and surgical procedures, and designed to develop information to protect the mother's health, and not designed to impede abortion, were found to be permissible.[1]

The prohibition of saline amniocentesis abortion was found to be invalid.[2,3]

The requirement of consent of the husband was found to be invalid.[3]

The requirement of parental consent (granting to the parents a "veto") was found to be invalid.[3,4]

The requirement that the physician must attempt to preserve the life of a fetus aborted in the first 12 weeks of pregnancy was found to be invalid.[3]

---

[1] Chief Justice Burger and Justices Brennan, Stewart, White, Marshall, Blackmun, Rehnquist, Powell, and Stevens heard the case. All of the Justices joined in these decisions.

[2] Justices Stewart and Powell agreed, if, as a matter of medical reality in a given community, the prohibition was in fact a prohibition of abortion.

[3] Justices White and Rehnquist dissented.

[4] Justice Stevens dissented.

Beal v. Doe, 432 U. S. 438 (1977)

Pennsylvania's refusal to extend Medicaid coverage for nontherapeutic abortions in the first trimester was found to be not inconsistent with federal Medicaid law.[1]

---

[1] Chief Justice Burger and Justices Stewart, White, Rehnquist, Powell, and Stevens joined in the decision. Justices Brennan, Marshall, and Blackmun dissented.

Maher v. Roe, 432 U. S. 464 (1977)

Connecticut's exclusion of Medicaid benefits for all abortions except those that are "medically necessary," a term defined by Connecticut to include psychiatric necessity, is not unconstitutional.[1]

---

[1] Chief Justice Burger and Justices Stewart, White, Rehnquist, Powell, and Stevens joined in the decision. Justices Brennan, Marshall, and Blackmun dissented.

Poelker v. Doe, 432 U. S. 519 (1977)

Challenges to a St. Louis, Missouri city ordinance led to the following decision:

The exclusion of abortion services from publicly financed hospitals is permissible.[1]

---

[1] Chief Justice Burger and Justices Stewart, White, Rehnquist, Powell, and Stevens joined in the decision. Justices Brennan, Marshall, and Blackmun dissented.

Colautti v. Franklin, 439 U. S. 379 (1979)

Challenges to a Pennsylvania statute led to the following decisions:

The requirement that a physician must make a determination "based on his experience, judgment, or professional competence" that if he or she has "sufficient reason to believe that the fetus may be viable," he or she must preserve the life of the fetus "so long as a different technique would not be necessary to preserve the life or health of the mother," was found to be vague and overbroad. It did not give the physician sufficient guidance as to whether the duty to the mother or to the fetus was paramount, "or whether it requires the physician to make a 'trade-off' between the woman's health and additional percentage points of fetal survival."

Also, the statute was found to be vague and overbroad because it could have been read so as to make a crime of a medical mistake which was made in good faith and without criminal intent.[1]

---

[1] Justices Brennan, Stewart, Marshall, Blackmun, Powell and Stevens joined in the decision. Chief Justice Burger and Justices White and Rehnquist dissented.

Bellotti v. Baird, 443 U. S. 622 (1979)

Challenges to a Massachusetts statute led to the following decisions:

The requirement that a minor under 18 obtain the consent of
both parents, and, if either would not give consent, seek a court order
showing "good cause," is invalid unless 1) the minor has the opportunity to show that she is sufficiently mature to make her own decision,
or 2) if she has the opportunity to show that the abortion was in her
best interest, before her parents were involved.[1]

---

[1] Chief Justice Burger and Justices Stewart, Rehnquist, and Powell joined in the decision. Justices
Brennan, Marshall, Blackmun, and Stevens concurred in the decision. Justice White dissented.

Harris v. Macrae, 448 U. S. 297 (1980)

The Court reviewed the Hyde Amendment to the Medicaid provisions of the Social Security Act and held that federal reimbursements for aboriton procedures may constitutionally be limited to the cost of those abortions which are medically necessary to save the life of the mother, or to pregnancies arising from rape or incest.[1]

---

[1] Chief Justice Burger and Justices Stewart, White, Rehnquist, and Powell joined in the decision. Justices Brennan, Marshall, Blackmun, and Stevens dissented.

Williams v. Zbaraz, 448 U. S. 358 (1980)

Challenges to an Illinois statute led to the following decision: Prohibition of medical assistance for all abortions except those necessary to save the life of the mother is constitutional.[1]

---

[1] Chief Justice Burger and Justices Stewart, White, Rehnquist, and Powell joined in the decision. Justices Brennan, Marshall, Blackmun, and Stevens dissented.

H. L. v. Matheson, Governor of Utah, 450 U. S. 398 (1981)

Challenges to a Utah Statute led to the following decision:

The requirement that the physician notify the parents "if possible" was found constitutional with respect to an unmarried minor girl who made no claim that she was mature and emancipated.[1]

---

[1] Chief Justice Burger and Justices Stewart, White, Rehnquist, Powell, and Stevens joined in the decision. Justices Marshall, Brennan, and Blackmun dissented.

City of Akron v. Akron Center for Reproductive Health, Inc., 462 U. S. 416 (1983)

An Akron, Ohio city ordinance led to the following decisions:

The requirement that all minors under the age of 15 obtain the consent of their parents was found to be invalid. With respect to the involvement of parents, the Court held that a parental veto was invalid; any minor, of any age, must be afforded the opportunity to present her claim, to a neutral tribunal, that she is sufficiently mature to make the abortion decision on her own.

The following requirements were found not to be reasonably related to maternal health and were therefore held to be invalid: All abortions in the second trimester must be performed in a hospital. The physician must communicate certain specific information regarding abortion and alternatives to abortion. (The requirement is invalid if the required information is designed to persuade against abortion, or if it details certain risks which the physician, in his or her judgment, determines to be inapplicable to a specific pregnancy.) All women seeking abortion must wait 24 hours.

The requirement that fetal remains be "disposed of in a humane and sanitary manner" was found to be too vague to give physicians reasonable notice of what was expected of them.[1]

---

[1] Chief Justice Burger and Justices Brennan, Marshall, Powell, Blackmun, and Stevens joined in the decision. Justices White, Rehnquist, and O'Connor dissented.

Planned Parenthood Association of Kansas City, Missouri v. Aschcraft, Attorney General of Missouri, 462 U. S. 476 (1983)

Challenges to a Missouri statute led to the following decisions:

The requirement that a minor gain parental consent was found permissible, if the statute provides procedures by which the minor can first show that she is sufficiently mature to make the decision on her own, and, if she is not sufficiently mature, if she can still show "good cause" to forego parental notice.

If a fetus is found to be viable, the requirement that a second physician attend the abortion procedure, in order to save the life of the child, is valid. (The first physician's primary responsibility would be the mother.)

The requirement that the pathologist's report, together with a copy of the tissue report, be filed with the hospital and State Board of health, is valid.[1]

---

[1] Chief Justice Burger and Justices Rehnquist, Powell, Stevens, and O'Connor joined in the decision. Justices Brennan, Marshall, Blackmun, and Stevens dissented.

Simopoulos v. Virginia, 462 U. S. 506 (1983)

Challenges to a Virginia statute led to the following decision:

The requirement that second trimester abortions which are not performed in a hospital be performed in an outpatient surgical clinic licensed by the State Department of Health is valid.[1]

---

[1] Chief Justice Burger and Justices Brennan, White, Marshall, Blackmun, Rehnquist, Powell, and O'Connor joined in the decision. Justice Stevens dissented on the ground that the statute was vague.

Thornburgh, Governor v. American College of Obstetricians and Gynecologists, 476 U. S. 747 (1986)

Challenges to a Pennsylvania statute led to the following decisions:

Record-keeping requirements which do not provide for confidentiality and which inquire into methods of payment were found invalid.

Requirements that a physician exercise a degree of care to preserve the life of the fetus as if the fetus were intended to be born alive and not aborted, and to use the abortion technique "which would provide the best opportunity for the unborn child to be born alive, unless . . . that method or technique would present a significantly greater medical risk to the life or health of the pregnant woman than would another available method or technique" were found invalid.

The requirement that a second physician attend the abortion of a fetus found to be viable, absent an exception for circumstances in which the mother might be endangered by delay in arrival of the second physician, was found to be invalid.[1]

---

[1] Justices Brennan, Marshall, Blackmun, Powell and Stevens joined in the decision. Chief Justice Burger and Justices White, Rehnquist, and O'Connor dissented.

Webster, Attorney General of Missouri v. Reproductive Health Services, 492 U. S. 490 (1989)

Challenges to a Missouri statute led to the following decision:

The Court held to be valid the requirement that a physician must perform certain specific tests of viability, including measurements of fetal age, weight, and lung capacity, if he or she believes that a fetus may be 20 or more weeks of gestational age, and it is the judgment of the physician that the tests are medically necessary in the given pregnancy. The requirement that the results of the tests be recorded in the mother's medical record was also held to be valid.[1]

---

[1] Chief Justice Rehnquist and Justices White and Kennedy joined in the decision. Justices O'Connor and Scalia concurred only in the judgment. Justices Brennan, Marshall, Blackmun, and Stevens dissented.

Planned Parenthood of Southeastern Pennsylvania v. Robert P. Casey, Docket Nos. 91-744, 91-902 (1992)

Challenges to a Pennsylvania statute led to the following decisions:

The essential holding of *Roe v. Wade* was retained and reaffirmed: 1) a woman has a right to an abortion before viability without undue interference from the State; 2) the State has a right to limit or prohibit abortion after viability if the law contains exceptions to save the life of the mother; and 3) the State has an important and legitimate interest in protecting maternal health and potential human life.

Roe's trimester framework was rejected. The Court concluded that the line should be drawn at viability, so that before that time the woman has a right to choose an abortion.

An "undue burden" standard was adopted to evaluate abortion restrictions. The Court concluded that a state regulation that places a substantial obstacle in the path of a woman seeking an abortion before viability imposes an undue burden on her right and is not valid.

Using this standard, the Court held that:

1) The requirement that a woman seeking an abortion give her informed consent prior to the procedure was found to be valid. The requirement that a physician disclose certain information about the abortion procedure and its risks and alternatives at least 24 hours prior to the procedure was also found to be valid. In addition, the statute required that a woman be informed about the availability of printed materials provided by the state and must receive them if she requests them.

2) A mandatory 24-hour waiting period between the provision of the information deemed necessary for informed consent and the performance of an abortion was also found to be valid.

3) The requirement that a minor seeking an abortion obtain the informed consent of one parent, or the consent of a judge if the minor cannot or does not wish to obtain the consent of a parent, was found to be valid.

4) Certain reporting requirements for clinics and other facilities that perform abortions were found to be valid.

5) The requirement that a married woman notify her husband of her intention to have an abortion was found to be invalid.[1,2]

---

[1] Justices O'Connor, Kennedy, and Souter announced the judgment of the Court. Chief Justice Rehnquist and Justices White, Blackmun, Stevens, Scalia, and Thomas concurred in part and dissented in part.

[2] A "medical emergency" would override the need to fulfill the other requirements of the statute (informed consent, 24-hour waiting period provisions, and the parental or judicial consent option for minors).

FROM *THE*
CONSTITUTION OF THE UNITED STATES

Preamble: We the People of the United States, in Order to form a more perfect Union, establish Justice, insure domestic Tranquility, provide for the common defence, promote the general Welfare, and secure the Blessings of Liberty to ourselves and our Posterity, do ordain and establish this Constitution for the United States of America.

First Amendment: Congress shall make no law respecting an establishment of religion, or prohibiting the free exercise thereof; or abridging the freedom of speech, or of the press; or the right of the people peaceably to assemble, and to petition the Government for a redress of grievances.

Fourth Amendment: The right of the people to be secure in their persons, houses, papers, and effects, against unreasonable searches and seizures, shall not be violated, and no Warrants shall issue, but upon probable cause, supported by Oath or affirmation, and particularly describing the place to be searched, and the persons or things to be seized.

Fifth Amendment: No person shall be held to answer for a capital, or otherwise infamous crime, unless on a presentment or indictment of a Grand Jury, except in cases arising in the land or naval forces, or in the Militia, when in actual service in time of War or public danger; nor shall any person be subject to the same offense to be twice put in jeopardy of life or limb; nor shall be compelled in any criminal case to be a witness against himself, nor be deprived of life, liberty, or property, without due process of law; nor shall private property be taken for public use, without just compensation.

Ninth Amendment: The enumeration in the Constitution, of certain rights, shall not be construed to deny or disparage others retained by the people.

Fourteenth Amendment: Section 1. All persons born or naturalized in the United States, and subject to the jurisdiction thereof, are citizens of the United States and of the State wherein they reside. No State shall make or enforce any law which shall abridge the privileges or immunities of citizens of the United States; nor shall any State deprive any person of life, liberty, or property, without due process of law; nor deny to any person within its jurisdiction the equal protection of the laws.

Justices of the Supreme Court,
1973–1992

The Justices of the Supreme Court of the United States, sitting at the time of the decisions of *Roe v. Wade* and *Doe v. Bolton*, were:

Chief Justice Warren E. Burger. Born September 17, 1907, in St. Paul, Minnesota. Studied at the University of Minnesota (1925–27); received his law degree from St. Paul (now Mitchell) College of Law (1931). Practiced law in St. Paul for many years, and taught at Mitchell.

Active in politics, Burger pledged the Minnesota delegation to President Dwight D. Eisenhower at the Republican National Convention in 1952. Appointed U.S. Assistant Attorney General by Eisenhower (1953). Served on U.S. Court of Appeals for the District of Columbia Circuit (1956–69). Nominated as fifteenth Chief Justice of the U.S. Supreme Court by Richard M. Nixon; took office on June 23, 1969. Retired from the Court in September 1986.

Associate Justice William O. Douglas. Born October 16, 1898, in Maine, Minnesota. Graduated from Whitman College in Washington (1920); received his law degree from Columbia University Law School (1925). Practiced law on Wall Street for one year; later taught at Columbia Law School (1928) and Yale Law School (until 1936).

Appointed member of the Securities Exchange Commission (1936); served as Chairman of S.E.C. (1937–39). Nominated to the U.S. Supreme Court by President Franklin D. Roosevelt; took office on April 17, 1939. Retired from the Court in 1975, after history's longest tenure as a Supreme Court Associate Justice (36 years, 7 months). A victim of polio, Douglas was nevertheless an avid outdoorsman; he wrote some 30 books, most on nature and conservation. Died January 19, 1980, in Washington, D.C.

Associate Justice William J. Brennan, Jr. Born April 25, 1906, in Newark, New Jersey. Received bachelor's degree from the University of Pennsylvania's Wharton School of Business (1928); received law degree from Harvard Law School (1931). Practiced law in Newark, specializing in labor law. Served as officer in U.S. Army in World War II (1942-45).

Served as Judge, New Jersey Superior Court (1949-51), and then Judge, Appellate Division (1951-52). Served on Supreme Court of New Jersey (1952-56). A Democrat, Douglas was nominated to the U.S. Supreme Court by Republican President Dwight D. Eisenhower. Took office on October 16, 1956. Retired from the Court in 1990.

Associate Justice Potter Stewart. Born January 23, 1915, in Jackson, Michigan. Received B.A. from Yale University (1937); studied at Oxford University, England (1937–38); received law degree from Yale University Law School (1941). During World War II, served as Lieutenant, U.S. Naval Reserve; awarded three battle stars. Practiced law in New York City and then Cincinnati, where he served on city council (1950–53) and as Vice Mayor (1952–53).

Appointed to the U.S. Court of Appeals for the Sixth Circuit by President Dwight D. Eisenhower in 1954, becoming the youngest Federal judge at that time. Nominated by Eisenhower to the U.S. Supreme Court; took office on October 14, 1958. Retired in 1981. Stewart then served as a member of the President's Commission on Central America, the President's Commission on Organized Crime, and the board of overseers of the Institute of Civil Justice. Died December 7, 1985, in Hanover, New Hampshire.

Associate Justice Byron R. White. Born June 8, 1917, in Fort Collins, Colorado. Received B.A. from the University of Colorado (1938); named All-American football player (1937). Studied at Oxford University, England, as a Rhodes Scholar (1939); received law degree from Yale Law School (1946). Served as U.S. Naval Reserve intelligence officer in Pacific during World War II (1941–46). Played professional football with the Pittsburgh Pirates (now Steelers) for one season (1938), and then with the Detroit Lions (1940–41) while attending law school. Inducted into the National Football Hall of Fame (1954).

Served as law clerk to U.S. Supreme Court Chief Justice Fred M. Vinson (1946–47). Practiced law in Denver, Colorado (1947–61). Member of the Presidential campaign staff of John F. Kennedy. Appointed Deputy Attorney General by Kennedy in 1961. Nominated to U.S. Supreme Court by Kennedy in 1962; took office on April 16, 1962.

Associate Justice Thurgood Marshall. Born July 2, 1908, in Baltimore, Maryland. Received A.B. from Lincoln University (1930); received law degree from Howard University (1933). Practiced law in Baltimore (1933–37). Served as Assistant Special Counsel, Special Counsel, and Director and Counsel for the legal defense and education fund of the National Association for the Advancement of Colored People (1936–61). Argued discrimination and school desegregation cases for the NAACP; won 29 of 32 cases he argued before the U.S. Supreme Court. Served on United States Court of Appeals for the Second Circuit (1961–65). Served as Solicitor General of the United States (1965–67). Appointed to the U.S. Supreme Court by President Lyndon B. Johnson; took office on October 2, 1967. First nonwhite to serve on the Court. Retired from the Court in 1991.

Associate Justice Harry A. Blackmun. Born November 12, 1908, in Nashville, Illinois. Received B.A. from Harvard University (1929); received law degree from Harvard Law School (1932). Practiced law in St. Paul, Minnesota (1934–50); then became resident counsel at the Mayo Clinic in Rochester, Minnesota. Taught at the St. Paul College of Law and the University of Minnesota Law School (1941–47).

Served on U.S. Court of Appeals for the Eighth Circuit (1959–70). Nominated to the U.S. Supreme Court by President Richard M. Nixon; took office on June 9, 1970.

Associate Justice William H. Rehnquist. Born October 1, 1924, in Milwaukee, Wisconsin. Received B.A. and M.A. from Stanford University (1948); received M.A. from Harvard University (1949); received law degree from Stanford University (1949). Served in Army Air Force in World War II. Served as law clerk to U.S. Supreme Court Associate Justice Robert H. Jackson (1952–53). Practiced law in Phoenix, Arizona (1953–69).

Served as U.S. Assistant Attorney General, heading the Office of Legal Counsel at the Department of Justice (1969–71). Appointed Associate Justice of the U.S. Supreme Court by President Richard M. Nixon; took office on January 7, 1972. Appointed by President Ronald W. Reagan as sixteenth Chief Justice of the U.S. Supreme Court; took office on September 26, 1986.

Associate Justice Lewis Franklin Powell, Jr. Born September 19, 1907, in Suffolk, Virginia. Received B.S. from Washington and Lee University (1929); received law degree from Washington and Lee (1931); received LL.M. from Harvard University (1932). Practiced law in Richmond, Virginia (1932-71). Served in Army Air Force in World War II, rising to rank of colonel; awarded Bronze Star, Legion of Merit, Croix de Guerre with palms. As chairman of the Richmond public school board (1952–1961) administered peaceful integration of city schools. Served as President of American Bar Association (1964–65), the American College of Trial Lawyers (1969–70), and the American Bar Foundation (1969–71).

Powell, a Democrat, was nominated to the U.S. Supreme Court by Republican President Richard M. Nixon; took office on February 7, 1972. Retired from the Court in 1987.

The current members of the U.S. Supreme Court, in addition to Chief Justice Rehnquist and Associate Justices White and Blackmun, are:

Associate Justice John Paul Stevens. Born April 20, 1920, in Chicago, Illinois. Received A.B. from the University of Chicago (1941); received law degree from Northwestern University (1947). Served in U.S. Navy during World War II; awarded Bronze Star. Served as law clerk for U.S. Supreme Court Associate Justice Wiley B. Rutledge (1947-48). Practiced law in Chicago (1948-70), specializing in antitrust law and serving on numerous public commissions. In 1969, served as a general counsel on a committee investigating misconduct by Illinois State Supreme Court justices.

Served on U.S. Court of Appeals for the Seventh Circuit in Chicago (1970-75). Appointed to U.S. Supreme Court by President Gerald R. Ford; took office on December 19, 1975.

Associate Justice Sandra Day O'Connor. Born March 26, 1930, in El Paso, Texas. Received A.B. from Stanford University (1950); received law degree from Stanford University (1952). Served as Deputy County Attorney in San Mateo, California (1952–53). Practiced law in Frankfurt, Germany (1954–57) and Phoenix, Arizona (1959–65). Served as Arizona Assistant Attorney General (1965–69). Held office as Arizona State Senator (1969–75); served as Republican Majority Leader (1973–74). Served as Judge, Maricopa County Superior Court (1975–79). Served on Arizona Court of Appeals (1979–81). Appointed to U.S. Supreme Court by President Ronald W. Reagan; took office on July 25, 1981; first woman to serve on the Court.

Associate Justice Antonin Scalia. Born March 11, 1936, in Trenton, New Jersey. Received A.B. from Georgetown University (1957); attended University of Fribourg, Switzerland (1955–56); received law degree from Harvard Law School (1960). Sheldon Fellow, Harvard University (1960-61). Practiced law in Cleveland, Ohio (1961–67). Served as Associate Professor of Law (1967–70) and Professor of Law (1970–74) at the University of Virginia. Served as General Counsel, Office of Telecommunications Policy, Executive Office of the President (1971–72); Chairman, Administrative Conference, U. S. (1972–74). Visiting Professor, Georgetown Law Center (1977); Stanford Law School (1980–81); Visiting Scholar, American Enterprise Institute (1977).

Served as Assistant Attorney General in the Office of Legal Counsel at the U.S. Department of Justice (1974–77). Served as Professor of Law, University of Chicago (1977–82). Served on U. S. Court of Appeals for the District of Columbia Circuit (1982–86). Appointed to the U. S. Supreme Court by President Ronald W.

Reagan; took office on September 26, 1986.

Associate Justice Anthony M. Kennedy. Born July 23, 1936, in Sacramento, California. Received A.B. from Stanford University (1958); attended London School of Economics; received law degree from Harvard Law School (1961). Practiced law in California (1961–75). Served as Professor of Constitutional Law at McGeorge School of Law, University of the Pacific (1967–75). Served on U.S. Court of Appeals for the Ninth Circuit (1976–88). Appointed to the U.S. Supreme Court by President Ronald W. Reagan; took office on February 18, 1988.

Associate Justice David H. Souter. Born September 17, 1939, in Melrose, Massachusetts. Received B.A. from Harvard University (1961); attended Oxford University, England, as Rhodes Scholar (1961–63); received law degree from Harvard Law School (1966). Practiced law in Concord, New Hampshire (1966–68). Served as Assistant Attorney General (1968–71); Deputy Attorney General (1971–76); Attorney General for State of New Hampshire (1976–78). Served on New Hampshire Superior Court (1978–83), then as Associate Justice of the New Hampshire Supreme Court (1983–90). Served on U.S. Court of Appeals for the First Circuit (1990). Appointed to the U.S. Supreme Court by President George Bush; took office on October 9, 1990.

Associate Justice Clarence Thomas. Born July 23, 1948, in Savannah, Georgia. Received B.A. from Holy Cross College (1970); received law degree from Yale Law School (1974). Served as Assistant Attorney General, State of Missouri (1974–77). Practiced law with Monsanto Company in St. Louis, Missouri (1977–79). Served as Legislative Assistant to U.S. Senator John C. Danforth (1979–81). Served as Assistant Secretary for Civil Rights, U.S. Department of Education (1981–82). Served as Chairman of the Equal Employment Opportunity Commission (1982–90). Served on U.S. Court of Appeals for the District of Columbia Circuit (1990). Appointed to the U.S. Supreme Court by President George Bush; took office on October 23, 1991.

GLOSSARY

abridgement of rights A reference to the provision of the Fourteenth Amendment that "No state shall make or enforce any law which shall abridge [deprive or reduce in scope] the privileges or immunities of citizens of the United States."

abstain, abstention The federal courts will often refrain from interfering with ongoing state proceedings and, as here, from ordering state authorities to comply with declared law, anticipating that State authorities will voluntarily comply. The doctrine of abstention grows out of comity between the federal and State governments.

ALI American Law Institute. An organization of legal scholars which publishes codifications of judicial precedents known as "Restatements," and which drafts uniform laws for the states. The ALI is not a governmental body, but its drafts of uniform laws have been adopted by many state legislatures. The ALI's "Restatements" are often treated as authority by the courts.

Amicus Curiae Latin for "friend of the court." *Amici* is the plural. A person or group with strong interests and views, but not actually a party to the case. *Amici* may submit legal briefs for the Supreme Court's consideration if they have the consent of all parties, or they may seek the permission of the Court.

appellant The party who appeals. The person who lost the case, or was dissatisfied with the result, in the lower court.

appellee The party against whom an appeal is made. The person who won the case or was satisfied with the result in the lower court.

brief The written presentations submitted by the parties for the Court's consideration. Briefs contain, among other things, statements of the facts which the advocate believes to be persuasive, citations to legal and other authorities, and reasoning.

canon law The ecclesiastical law of the Roman Catholic Church.

Coke Sir Edward Coke (pronounced "Cook"), 1552–1634. English Lord, lawyer, scholar, and writer, known especially for his four-volume *Institutes* (1628), which are often cited as authority regarding the dictates of the early Common Law.

Common Law The body of law and principles, usages and customs, including judicial precedents, of England and the American colonies before the American Revolution. Each of the states, with the exception of Louisiana, adopted the common law, to the extent that it was not in conflict with the federal or state constitution or laws.

Complaint See **pleadings**

concurred, concurring A Justice agreed with the decision, but reached the decision by different or additional reasoning. Often, a Justice who concurs writes a separate, concurring opinion.

declaratory judgment, declarative relief A party may request a court for an order which will remove doubt as to his or her legal position, without at the same time asking for an injunction or for money damages. There must be an actual controversy, and the circumstances which might lead to injury must be on the horizon. The order, or judgment, if it is granted, will "declare" the rights of the parties, and it will bind their future dealings. (Ordinarily, a request for a declaratory order is accompanied by a request for an injunction.)

dictum, dicta An observation or remark by a judge, in an opinion, of his or her understanding of a point of law which is not necessarily involved in the controversy before the judges. A dictum does not carry the authority which is carried by a statement about a point of law which goes to the heart of the controversy which is the subject of the opinion.

dissented, dissenting   A Justice disagreed with the decision. Usually, Justices who dissent write a separate, dissenting opinion.

Due Process Clause   A reference to the provision of the Fourteenth Amendment that states "...nor shall any State deprive any person of life, liberty, or property, without due process of law;..."

equal protection   A reference to the provision of the Fourteenth Amendment that "No state shall...deny to any person within its jurisdiction the equal protection of the laws."

et al.   An abbreviation for the Latin *et alia,* which means "and others."

guardian ad litem   A person who is appointed by the Court, in a specific lawsuit, to protect the interests of a minor or an incompetent person.

Id.   An abbreviation for the Latin idem, which means "the same thing." Used rather than repeating a part of a citation which has recently appeared in full in the text.

injunction, injunctive relief   A court order forbidding someone from doing something or commanding someone to do something, as opposed to an order awarding money damages.

interrogatories   During the pre-trial stages of a civil case, one party may pose a series of written questions called interrogatories to his opponent. They must be answered under oath. They may be used to discover information in the hands of the adversary, or to pin down the case.

intervene, intervenor　An intervenor is a person who comes into a case after it has been started by other parties. An intervenor must have an interest in the case which might be impaired or impeded by a court's judgment, or there must be claims or defenses in the case which has already been started which share common legal or factual issues with the intervenor's claims or defenses.

judicial notice　In federal courts, the introduction and use of evidence is governed by the Federal Rules of Evidence. For the most part, these rules require that all evidence must come into the case through a witness who has taken the oath and subjected himself or herself to cross-examination. There are some exceptions. One of the exceptions is that the court may take "judicial notice" of facts which are not subject to reasonable dispute, and which are capable of accurate and ready determination by referral to sources whose accuracy cannot reasonably be questioned. Parties in a case have the opportunity to object to "notice" of facts which they consider unsubstantiated or inaccurate.

Justiciable, justiciability　This concept embodies the notion that not all controversies are amenable to judicial intervention or solution. Courts are usually most comfortable, and feel it to be in keeping with their expertise, to answer focused, "yes or no" questions—("Is the defendant guilty?" "Should the behavior be enjoined?" "Is the defendant liable?")—or to calculate damages. Courts tend to feel uncomfortable forging solutions which call for selection from a variety of options. Such programmatic efforts are the day-to-work of legislatures. (However, in a decision which many court-watchers feel is one of the most significant of the Supreme Court's history, and over strong objections of non-justiciability, the Court did take upon itself the task of supervising the reapportionment of voting districts.) There are situations where the concepts of justiciability and standing appear to overlap, and this case may be one of them. See **standing**

lenity　Forbearance, charity, clemency, humanness.

misprision　In this context, a misdemeanor.

moot   Because of the passage of time and changes in circumstances, the controversy no longer exists (has "become moot").

narrowly drawn   It is an accepted rule of interpreting the meaning of a criminal statute that the statute be narrowly drawn. That is, if the words of the statute could be read to have more than one meaning, the statute must be given the meaning which is least restrictive of behavior, and which does not infringe constitutionally protected rights. The statute might be subject to so many interpretations that it is "vague." See **vague**

notice   See **judicial notice**

overbroad   A criminal statute is overbroad if it forbids constitutionally protected behavior. For example, some statutes which regulate the use of public areas have been struck down as infringing the right of free speech.

penumbras   a word often used with a special meaning in opinions which interpret the Bill of Rights and the Due Process Clause of the Fourteenth Amendment. The words "emanations" and "periphery" are used in the same contexts. The words refer to rights which are not specifically enumerated in the Bill of Rights, but which are necessarily implied in order to make the specifically enumerated rights meaningful. For example, the freedom of the press, which is specifically enumerated in the First Amendment, has been held to imply and to protect the freedoms to distribute, to teach, to inquire, and to think.

peripheral, periphery   See **penumbras**

pleadings   The papers filed in a civil case, usually in the early stages, which set forth the claims of the plaintiff, and the defenses of the defendant. They are known as the Complaint and the Answer. In the federal courts, pleadings are supposed to be "short and plain." There are additional pleadings in cases with multiple parties.

police power   The phrase is used here with a broader meaning than the "power of the police force." The police power is the power of a state to adopt laws and regulations and to delegate the power of enforcement in order to insure the general welfare and the rights and privileges of its citizens. The police power is subject to the limitations of the federal and state constitutions.

procedural due process   See substantive due process.

received   Adopted.

standing   A person must have "standing," that is, a sufficient personal stake in the controversy, to entitle him or her to the attention of a court. To have standing, a person must be injured or threatened with injury, as distinguished from an interested bystander. The requirement of "standing" insures that the adversaries will pursue their positions with zeal, and that they are the right people to fight the battle, since legal rights will be determined and law may be announced.

substantive due process   "Substantive due process" and "procedural due process" are phrases which have been used in controversies concerning the meaning and scope of the Due Process Clause of the Fourteenth Amendment. Many of the Justices, during the Court's history, and in these opinions, have taken different positions on the meaning and the significance of these phrases.

To suggest some of the issues: Earlier in this century, the Supreme Court dealt with attempts by legislatures to provide economic reforms, such as maximum hours and minimum wages. The Court originally held that certain of these statutes were invalid, under the Fourteenth Amendment. Dissenters in those cases, who later were vindicated, wrote that it was not the job of the Supreme Court to become a "superlegislature"—to place its wisdom above that of the legislatures by writing "substance" into the Constitution which was not intended by the framers.

Everyone agrees that the Due Process Clause establishes "procedural" safeguards. For example, the right to the assistance of counsel and to a speedy trial are a guaranteed part of the procedures in state criminal cases. However, virtually no one argues that the Clause provides only "procedural" safeguards. It is well established, for example, that a state government may not take private property for public use without just compensation.

The Bill of Rights—the first ten Amendments of the Constitution—was adopted to limit the power of the *federal* government. The Due Process Clause was part of a Civil War Amendment which placed limitations on the power of *state* governments. One area of Constitutional controversy is whether the Due Process Clause was intended to make some, all, none, and/or provisions in addition to, the provisions of the Bill of Rights applicable to the states.

Justices tend to use the phrase "substantive due process" when they disapprove of an attempt to find a "right" in the Due Process Clause. There does not seem to be a word or phrase that the Justices use to describe those rights which the Constitution provides, but which are not "procedural." This is not to say that the Justices feel they need to find such a catchphrase to express the basis of a decision.

supra   Above in the text.

tort law   A tort is a "wrong." Tort law is the law of private or civil wrongs, which are actionable in the court. Torts include assault and battery, false imprisonment, theft, trespass, fraud, libel and slander, negligence, outrage, pollution, and wrongful prosecution. The acts which give rise to a tort, if they are intentional, may also give rise to a criminal prosecution.

vague, vagueness   A criminal statute is unconstitutional if its meaning is vague and unclear, and fails to give fair notice, to a person of ordinary intelligence, that his contemplated behavior is forbidden. Persons should not have to guess whether or not they are breaking the law. Also, a vague statute encourages arbitrary and erratic arrests and convictions. For example, "vagrancy" ordinances have been struck down as vague.

viz.   Abbreviation for the Latin *videlicet*, which means "namely," or "that is to say," or "to wit."

ABOUT THE AUTHOR

Bo Schambelan annotated the texts of the opinions in *Roe v. Wade* and
Doe v. Bolton, and prepared the Glossary, Postscript, and the biogra-
phies of the Justices. Mr. Schambelan received his undergraduate
degree from Haverford College in 1961 and his law degree from
Harvard Law School in 1964. He has practiced trial and appellate law
in the state and federal courts for more than twenty-five years.